The private journal and diary of John H. Surratt, the conspirator - Primary Source Edition

John H. 1844-1916 Surratt

Price, 25 Cents.

PRIVATE
Journal & Diary (of)
OHN H. SURRATT

HE CONSPIRATOR

THE PRIVATE
JOURNAL and DIARY

OF

JOHN H. SURRATT,

THE CONSPIRATOR.

EDITED AND ARRANGED BY

DION HACO, Esq.

"Murder most foul."
Shakespeare.

NEW YORK:
FREDERIC A. BRADY, PUBLISHER,
22 ANN STREET, near NASSAU.

JOHN H. SURRATT'S PRIVATE DIARY.

CHAPTER I.

A MYSTERY ELUCIDATED.

July 3, 1860.—Well, at last it is over, and I am fairly in it! Am I satisfied? Perhaps, yes; it may-be, no! My darling wish—the principal topic of my waking thoughts—my ever haunting nightly dreams—my heart's most earnest desire—oh! the craving I for so long a time have had to expore the hidden mysteries of that—I dare not name it—has at last been gratified. And, oh! what an experience!

Last evening—I shudder as I think of it—will be one of the few most important—perhaps the most moment-ous of the epochs of my heretofore unknown life; and, having chosen my path, must follow it to the end, for the road is open. Still I am yet in the dark; and I have to learn, and must know more.

Solemn, very solemn, indeed, was the occasion— horribly binding that obligation—fearfully terrible the penalty; but it is over now, and I know the secret— at least, am acquainted with some of the awful myste-ries which overshadow the whole.

What a crowd! what a congregation! The outside world would never believe that, in that dark room, there were to have been found men of all grades of society. But it is true; and the mighty machine, when it begins to move, will permeate through all the stratas of official life. Cabinet members, high in office, were

1

there; and so, also, the unsuccessful actors, who seek elsewhere the fame they failed to secure on the mimic stage—eminent Judges, who now, by their decisions, influence the destinies of the nation; and editors, who wield a mightier weapon than the sword, and hold a lever that moves the world—Congressmen, who pretend to make our laws; and roughs, who never fail to break them. All these were there, for I saw them. It was a strange union of opposing elements; but they all have their part to play in the drama of the "Coming Future," and I, among the number.

I saw, there, many a familiar face, both of politician and prize-fighter; those who frequent the National Capital during the sessions of Congress, hang around the great halls of National Legislation, and appear daily in such style on Pennsylvania Avenue. John asserts that every one of these men will yet be needed; for, in the great cause, all are equal, and they will each have their respective work to do. Had I but been told one-half of what is now known to me, it would have then seemed a fallacy, an impossibility. Were I still at College, it would seem to me as if I had been a victim of some trick from my fellow collegiates.

But is it all true? Yes, terribly true!

One thing, however, is still fresh in my remembrance, vividly so—"I must neither write nor speak upon or about what I see or hear." No eye can see me now, none other than mine will ever peruse these lines; therefore, should I make a record of what I have learned, it cannot be of any injury to my friends or the cause.

But a thought has just flashed across my mind— Why should I, with such a fearful warning, and terrible peril of the penalty before my mental vision, write a single word about last night's work? Why risk the chance of so important a paper falling into any other other person's hands? But can I not prevent any such mischance? Yes, certainly; it can be hidden.

Should this old house be destroyed, my labor may be in vain; but it shall never fall in the hands of an enemy.

This is a very lonely place, and some employment is necessary, wherewith to occupy my mind; otherwise, my anxiety will get the better of my reason, and I shall go crazy. Why does mother live here? Why will she not live in the city? Surely, there cannot be so many attractions in Surrattsville, that she should give up every comfort for the mere pleasure of residing in a place called by our name. If she can see anything charming in it, I do not; and I would willingly exchange all that may be enticing—according to her ideas—for a good frolic in Washington, with those who are of my own turn of mind. Still, the time may come when some important change will and must take place; for if the cause succeeds—and succeed it must with such excellent plans—the name I bear will become as famous as any in history. Then, indeed, will this record prove valuable; for it will show those in power that I was with them at the beginning, and kept true to the end. If it prove but this, my diary will not have been kept in vain.

I was in Washington, yesterday morning, waiting, in anxious expectation, for the hour to arrive that was to make me a wiser if not a greater man. At half past twelve, yesterday afternoon, my friend came for me, and we went together to the depot. He had very often spoken to me of what he had discovered, and did so even yesterday, as we were walking along; but yet he would give no more information than would serve to inflame my curiosity. That man is destined for a brilliant career; his ambition for fame is overpowering, and appears never to be satisfied. He is certain to make for himself a name in history; and he would almost refuse to die without it. How I envy him!

We got on board the cars for the monumental city;

for it was there that I was to be instructed, and there I received—but my pen is too rapid for a mere simple record.

How slow steam is for anxious minds! I would,
yesterday, have travelled by electricity, so anxious was
I to learn those terrible secrets, and the laggard
wheels appeared to revolve as slowly as those of the
old wagon in by-gone times. Never did the ride seem
so long and tedious, as during yesterday afternoon.

But at length we arrived at the end of our journey,
and were in the city of Baltimore.

Shall I ever forget that large house on Monument
Square? I think not. On the outside, it had all the
appearance of a fashionable dwelling, and the thousands
that daily passed it by, never dreamed that in that
stately, yet quiet building, were enacted the scenes I
last night witnessed.

It was not dark when we arrived—the meetings
were held in broad daylight, doubtless in conseqence,
that midnight meetings would have brought around
us some of those lynx-eyed myrmidons who are always
ready when they are not wanted—and instantaneously
my companion ascended the steps. A slight push, and
the door, to my great surprise, flew open immediately;
but, beyond, and barring our further progress, was a
half-glass hall door covered, on the inside, with a close,
thick lace curtain. As this is far from an uncommon
circumstance with all respectable houses, it did not
pointedly attract my attention until after the following
strange things had transpired.

Strict silence was enjoined on me by a sign from my
friend, and I at once became as mute as death.

A tap on the glass was next given—peculiar and
significant was that signal—which was readily answered from within. The heavy lace across the pane prevented my seeing anyone, although some person, on
the watch, was apparently there. A third rap, soft,
slight, yet certain, was given from without; then, with
a jerk, the door flew wide open.

The space beyond was vacant, and we passed at once within.

A death-like silence reigned around, and seemed to fill me with dread.

Where was the watcher? He could not anywhere be seen. How had he so quickly disappeared? No door was observable except the one by which we had entered; and yet the being who had answered the signal was certainly not there. The only observable object was a series of carpeted stairs, which we, after closing the door, quietly and silently ascended, to the head of the first flight. At this place our path was blocked by a panelled wainscoting—the object of which I could not then divine. Our further movements seemed absolutely checked by an insurmountable obstacle. My friend and guide, however, appeared to know the secret; and, after an interchange of signal knocks, a panel flew open, and we passed through.

The next moment the panel was again closed, and we were in darkness.

I felt the chill of steel against my hand and face, and the next moment a sharp point of some weapon slightly pierced my breast. With a shudder I drew back, when a deep voice said,

"Those who would pass here must face both fire and steel."

"We are willing to face both—for Liberty," answered my friend.

"It shall be ours," replied the voice. "Pass!"

My hand was taken by someone (who, I know not,) and I was led, in the darkness, through what seemed to be an interminable passage, at the end of which was a door, which, as I approached, instantly flew open, apparently without cause or human aid.

"Advance," said the voice, in a commanding tone.

I moved forward, but not without some amount of nervous agitation.

The door closed behind me, and I found myself in a large apartment, alone.

"Where had my companion gone?" was the thought which naturally flashed across my mind. He had left me alone, in that strange and mysterious place, without one clue to guide my actions, or any one near of whom I could ask directions or request assistance. "What could I do? and where really was I?"

Finding myself standing alone in that apaatment, the feeling naturally arose in my mind that it would be more pleasant to be seated; and finding every convenience therefore, I carelessly threw myself on a lounge to await the coming of my companion.

While waiting, my eyes naturally wandered around the place, which appeared to be a handsome drawing-room, or something of that character, and was fitted up in a most elegant style. It seemed to be about fifty feet in length, by about thirty feet deep, in the form of an oblong square, one of the longer sides apparently facing the street, upon which a half dozen windows opened, in the most natural manner. There was no mystery on that side of the room. Between each of the windows hung a pier glass, of large dimensions, in heavy gilt frames, and had, apparently, not been removed from their places for years. Heavy curtains, partially covered the windows, but not enough to keep out the light, which flooded the apartment under the genial influence of the brightly shing sun. All this my vision embraced at a glance.

The remaining walls now engaged my attention, and I then noticed that they were all covered with a rich paper, ornamented with a simple ring of gilt at regular intervals. Pictures hung from ceiling to floor, many of them painted on canvass and stretched within handsome frames, being suspended by heavy bullion cords and tassels, and representing full length and life size portraits of noted men, among whom may be reckoned Calhoun, Pierce, Secretary Davis, and others;

together with representations of important events in our history, as a country, during the revolutionary period. The arms of the Southern States were also represented in illuminated coloring; but I saw none belonging to the Free States. A grand gaselier was hung suspended from the ceiling, and, on the blue painted ceiling, was traced in gold, a large and brilliant ring, passing entirely around the filigree work which concealed the place where the plain pipe became united with the pendant. All this I soon observed, and began to tire of my silent examination.

At last my attention was directed to the fact that not a door appeared to open from this apartment, with the exception of the one by which I had entered, and it now became a matter of mental wonder why and with what object I had been placed in this room, which seemed to lead to nowhere beyond. The absence of my friend, also, greatly perplexed me.

[Here the writer appears to have been disturbed, as the diary is broken off at this place; and, when renewed, the style of the handwriting and the color of the ink is somewhat changed, as if he had allowed an interval of time to elapse, before re-commencing the record. Other entries, relating to simple family matters, and under various dates, had, certainly, meanwhile been made; but as they have no connection with the thread of the important part of the writing—his connection with the conspiracy—it has been deemed advisable to omit them, both here and throughout the remainder of the work. In a book of this character, where space is limited, it is necessary to condense as much as possible, without destroying the purity of the original; and, although many would like to see what Surratt has to say about his own family, it has been deemed advisable to erase such matters from this edition. Should circumstances warrant the issue of a larger work, these entries might then be given.— EDITOR.]

CHAPTER II.

MORE ABOUT THE MYSTERY.

Hesitation is bad, procrastination is worse. I had begun to write about my visit to Baltimore, and, since leaving off, have been but little inclined to renew the theme. But what is the use of keeping a diary unless everything is put down? Therefore, as I have begun my private history, it may as well be made as perfect as possible.

It might have been an hour, or only twenty minutes, that I had waited alone in that room; but, as I took no account of the time, it seemed almost an age. Every feature of the apartment had been examined, and I could have described every color therein, from the paper on the walls, and the hangings of the windows to the uniforms of the revolutionary heroes, and the background of the portraits. Still no one came, and the solitude became painful.

"Can this have been a deception?" thought I; "and has the trip from Washington to this place been made only to play a trick upon me?"

Patience is a virtue, but still it may at times be overtested; and, certainly, on this occasion, it required a great deal of it to reconcile me to remain (alone so long.) Young and impetuous, I wished to know the secret; but, at the same, I had no desire to be kept there in that manner—especially, as it might after all only prove a trick, a practical joke of my friends playing. This thought first excited me, then vexed, and finally made me mad; and, in an instant, starting to my feet, I rushed to the door by which I had entered the room. Useless—it was fastened.

"There is no help for it," thought I; "therefore the best thing to do, is to wait and abide the result."

The longer I had to wait, the more nervous I became; until at last my patience was entirely exhausted, and a nameless dread took its place. The salutations in the dark rushed to my memory; and the thought of facing fire and steel, to find out a secret that might in the end only prove worthless, was not entirely pleasant, even to me who never flinched from any known or open danger.

While in this state of mind I heard a voice, from some invisible form, say:

"Arise, and follow, if you would be made acquainted with the secrets of the Knights of the Golden Circle."

Without delay I sprang to my feet, but my guide was still not to be seen—at least, I had not yet observed him, although certain that the speaker must have been in the room when giving me the order to get up from my seat.

Suddenly the room grew dark, and I became aware of the fact that, by some unaccountable means, the heavy curtains had dropped before the windows, and had thus excluded the light. The next moment my hands were seized on either side, each by a strong and gauntleted grasp, and an unknown and unseen person next placed a bandage over my eyes. Then my clothing was torn from my breast, which was thus bared; and held and blinded, I was led from the room—whither, I knew not, and have not since divined. There seemed to be no end to the long path, if path it was; and the doors that were opened and closed were so numerous that all attempt at counting their numbers was soon given up by me.

At length we stopped before a door—at least, such I judged it to be, from the signal given upon it and returned from the other side—and the following question was asked in a military tone of voice;

"Who comes here?"

"One who is true to our cause," was the reply of one near me.

"How is he known to be true?" was the question next uttered by the first voice.

"By the recommendation of a tried knight," replied my supposed guide, for the voice was strange to my ears, as indeed were they all.

"He can then be trusted?" were the next words uttered.

"Such is our belief," was the reply.

"But should he fail, and betray us—what then?"

"He will learn the penalty soon enough."

"Advance."

We moved onward a few steps, when the same cold contact with steel, and the same sharp but slight puncture of the breast, was felt, as on a former occasion. This time I did not flinch, although the sharp pain was as unexpected as before. Again I heard a solemn voice utter, in a slow and measured tone, the ominous words:

"Those who would pass here must face both fire and steel."

"Are you willing to do so?" asked another, addressing me.

Having, after a few moment's consideration, answered in the affirmative, I was again told to advance, and commanded to kneel, on what seemed to be a cushion, as it yielded slightly to the pressure of my knee.

While in this position, an oath, terrible, horrible and appalling, was administered by the same solemn voice, and, while kneeling, I had to repeat the words after him in a slow and distinct tone, one hand resting on something cold as ice, the other on a book which appeared to be open.

The obligations taken, I was then informed that it would be necessary to remember every word I had uttered—can I ever forget them?—and not to forget the penalty of a disclosure of what I should learn, or a betrayal of the names of any one with whom I should be brought into companionship, no matter when, where, or under what pain, peril or promise. I was also admonished never to allude, either publicly or privately, to what I might then or hereafter learn; always to be ready to assist a brother-knight, even unto death; to abide by and follow all the directions of the order with which I had become connected; to carry out the objects which should be subsequently communicated to me, if found worthy of confidence; to bear witness and even to swear falsely in order to save a brother's life or liberty, if arrested for anything appertaining to the directions of the order; never to give a verdict against a brother, if on a jury to try him for any offense arising from directions emanating from the order, or any of its officers; and, in every way, to make the business of the new body, to which I had become allied, pre-eminent before religion, political feeling, parental or fraternal duty, or even before love of country. It was to be first and foremost in everything, at daylight or midnight, at home or abroad, before the law of the land or the affection for a wife, mother or child; to be all and everything.

"Are you willing to abide by this obligation?" asked the voice.

What could I do, or say? Refuse, I dare not; for I had felt the sharp point of the sword at my breast, and the words of that horrible oath still rang in my ears and vibrated through my aching brain. I was powerless to refuse, and therefore answered—faintly, it is true—in the affirmative.

"You remember the penalty?" asked the voice.

Could I have ever forgotten it? Remember it? Yes, indeed, did I remember it; perhaps, too vividly for the calm reflection of my mind at that moment. The very question, calling up, as it did, the rememberance, made me silent for the time, and I could not give a reply.

"Brother Knights!" exclaimed the voice, in a solemn tone, "Recall to the mind of him who now kneels here, the penalty of betrayal, either by sign, word or deed."

A sound like thunder rang around me; the clanging of arms broke the former almost death-like silence, and a hundred or more voices murmured, hissed, whispered or groaned out, three times, the single word,

"*Death!* DEATH!! DEATH!!!"

The first sound was horrible in its solemnity; the second utterance was terrible in its significance; the third and last was appalling in the repetition and the grave-like silence which followed it. My senses almost reeled under the influence of the fearful warning; my tongue appeared to swell until it filled my mouth and nearly choked me; I felt the hot blood rush over my brain and burn as it pursued its rapid course; it seemed as if the tortures of all the infernal regions had come upon me in a moment; I thought madness would be the result, unless the trial was soon to be ended, and yet I could not speak. And all this time my eyes were bandaged and my limbs bound. It was not the fear of death that caused within such terror— for I was willing to face any danger that could be seen; it was not the binding obligation I had taken— for I had firmly resolved to be true; but the nameless, unknown and unseen perils of that place and from those around me, appeared to call up to my imagination a thousand fears, indistinct and shadowy, yet plain enough to my mental vision. I had longed, craved for and enrnestly desired to obtain a secret; but would, at that moment, have given up all I then possessed, or ever hoped to gain, could I have safely withdrawn from the " Circle " within which I found myself so inextricably enclosed. Shall I, can I ever forget that time, those few, long moments of agony? Never; no not while life remains within this body, or until my senses become benumbed with the frosts of age or imbecility. Never!

How long the silence lasted, I know not; but the

same solemn voice—it seemed miles away, and yet was plainly distinct—again addressed me in a slow manner, first repeating the awful word that had been repeated by so many voices, then admonishing me never to forget it, and finally inquiring whether I was ready to proceed with my initiation. I could return no verbal answer—my tongue refused its office—and I merely bowed my head, more mechanical than otherwise, for, to my present remembrance, it does not appear that I had any voluntary power left within my body.

"It is well," said the voice. "Proceed!"

A movement of feet was next heard by me, followed by a low murmur of voices; the words uttered were drowned by the one single sound that burned through my brain, rang in my ears, appeared in letters of blood before my blinded eyes, and was present to me in every possible shape. That word was,

"DEATH."

The movements and sounds all ceased, and the solemn silence again ensued, which after a short interval was broken by the voice I had before heard, saying,

"Show him all."

A chorus of voices repeated the words, and the next instant the bandage was quickly taken from my eyes. For a few seconds my vision was blinded by the light, the dazzling light that fell upon me at that moment; and, before I could recover from the strain thus inflicted upon those organs of sight, I felt a number of sharp points pierce my breast, back and sides. My right hand had become almost frozen with the cold object upon which it rested, while the remainder of my body was in a perfect fever. I gave one glance around me, and, amid what appeared to be a cloud of fire, stood a number of armed men, clothed in coats of mail, their helmeted heads surmounted by red and white feathers, and their faces covered with barred vizors of metallic plates. Each had a sword in his hand, and every one of the points were directed at my almost paralyzed body, puncturing the flesh, and causing the smarts I had so recently felt.

Gradually my sight became restored, and, one by one, the objects before and around me were visible. The mailed knights stood as still as statues, and any movement of mine might have caused a serious if not a deadly wound from one or the other of their weapons, which shone with a bright, glaring and flashing brilliancy on every side. Had I desired it ever so much, movement or escape was an impossibility.

The light next appeared to become, through some invisible agency, slowly, very slowly of a dimmer character, and to burn with less radiance and dazzling glare; but whether this was actually the case, or some optical illusion, I am now at a loss to determine. I then perceived for the first time that I was kneeling before an an altar on which burned a dull blue flame; that my left hand had rested on an open Bible, and my right—horror of horrors—on the face of a corpse.

" *Death!*"

How the word rang in my ears. With a horrifying glance I looked down towards the floor, and beheld another corpse, upon whose breast I had been compelled to kneel.

" DEATH!!"

Again the word rang in my ears. I raised my eyes to those around, saw no glance of encouragement beyond those helmeted faces, and could comprehend nothing but the bright, polished swords, presented at me on every side.

" DEATH!!!"

Still that pitiless word was present. A mailed knight stood beyond the altar, in the direction from which I had heard that solemn voice, and with his unsheathed sword he pointed silently to the ghastly object on which my right hand rested. Not a word emanated from his lips, but his sword's point echoed the appalling, terrible word,

"*DEATH!*"

Darkness appeared to spread itself before my vision. I felt my senses leaving me, and a nameless horror took possession of my whole soul.

I saw and knew nothing more!

[Here again the record is broken by the entry of unimportant items, among which are such things as allusions to the approaching elections, but without any comments worthy of note. The writer seemed to think that the day was not lost until the final result was announced, and then his diary again becomes of interest to the reader.—EDITOR.]

CHAPTER III.

THE ELECTION AND WHAT FOLLOWED.

November 7, 1860.—So the railsplitter has been elected. Then our work is really to begin. I feared it, but hoped that there would have been no reason for trouble; that there would have arisen no real cause for dividing the country. Yet it must now come, and will come, for I am too well assured the South will not allow itself to be ruled by a Black Republican. Not a single slave State has given him a vote, and yet he is elected. The balance of power has gone; our party is no longer the unit it was; in spite of the ramifications of that great order to which I belong, the power has slipped from our grasp, and without doubt the Slave States will all go out of the Union. They are fully prepared for it, and New York will join us—at least the "Herald" says so. The work will now begin, and we are sure to gain our point, as some of those now in power are on our side, and the work of separation will in a great measure take place before the new party comes in. All is prepared, and *we* are ready.

December 24, 1860.—The work has begun in earnest. South Carolina is out of the Union. First in every-thing, she leads the way to glory. I wish it had been the good State of Maryland. But, although ready for the work, her time is not yet come. We may control events; but cannot alter time as it is. But Maryland is all right, and, so are the rest of the States. We can also count upon New York and San Francisco. The work begins well.

New Year's Day, 1861.—I made several calls to-day, and met many of the Knights. This calling serves more purposes than merely paying ceremonious visits. I heard some strange whispers among the ladies, and am not yet sure but that the present Administration may be compelled to hold for want of a constitutional successor. Such things have happened, and who knows what may again happen.

January 3, 1861.—Visited Baltimore yesterday. Had a grand meeting. Several of the northern cities represented. Delegates said the Knights were only waiting for orders. They asserted the failure of the elections was a foregone conclusion; but that New York did her duty bravely. The fault lay with the State politicians. She was, however, ready to act at the proper time, and would prove true to the South, as her interest lay in that direction. The navy yard, would, if required, be in the hands of those who could control matters; and, therefore, no war could be de-clared against the South; while she would, virtually, hold all the government works by means of the action of the Knights. Half the army and navy officers are members; so the work goes bravely on.

[The remainder of the entries during the month of January are short and concise, and refer entirely to

private matters, with the exception of the simple record of the separation or secession of the various States
of the Southern Confederacy, and the repeated remark
that " the work goes bravely on." No very pointed
allusion is made to Lincoln, personally ; neither are
there recorded any words of anger or dislike to the
Republican party. Caution, in writing, seems to have,
at this time, guided his pen, and the record is therefore plain and simple and without comment.—
EDITOR].

February 4, 1861.—The Southern States are forming
themselves into a separate Confederacy, and making
a new republic of their own. But Maryland does not
seem willing to join in the movement, although Baltimore is all right. In some way or the other there is
an undercurrent in the country parts against us. The
Knights are working well, and are using all their influence to change the political feeling ; but, although the
majority think the South right, they do not feel inclined to join. We are sure, at any rate, of a majority
in the Legislature, and the State must go out. Then
my fortune will be made, for the Black Republicans
will never dare to force us to remain in the Union
against our will. And the birthday of Washington
is to be natal day of our new Confederacy—as good
an omen as it is national and loyal. The delegates
met to-day, at Montgomery, to organize the new government.

February 9, 1861.—The Constitution has been
adopted, and Jefferson Davis has been declared President. See how the order works. Our principal
leader has been chosen our Executive chief. I am
sorry they selected Stevens for Vice President—he's not
true to the core. When is my turn to come to get
some of these honors ?

February 12, 1861.—Lincoln started yesterday from
Springfield. We met yesterday in Baltimore. That's
a strange coincidence. Well, perhaps what we did

and what we have resolved to do, may be pregnant with great results. Who knows what may happen before Lincoln gets to Washington—if he ever gets there.

February 18, 1861.—President Davis was inaugurated to-day in the Confederate capital. Hurrah for Davis! Three groans for Lincoln and all the Black Republican crew.

February 19, 1861.—So Lincoln has reached New York in safety. What are they all doing? Surely they could contrive some scheme to have upset the train, or something else, to prevent his ever reaching Washington. Should he fail to reach Washington, it will be all the better; but it has firmly been resolved that the Northern rail splitter shall never be inaugurated in that city where Southern gentlemen have heretofore directed the affairs of the nation. We have possession of all the Southern arsenals, thanks to the agency of our famous order, and we will also, at the proper time, have the Capital within our limits. We could easily take it now, but it will be better to take the Black Republican party with the city. What a day that will be, when we, of Maryland, proclaim to the South that the noble city of Washington is hers, and can be held by her as the Capital of the Southern Confederacy. It is all prepared.

February 20, 1861.—Booth called on me to-day. He gave me a glowing account of his visit to Richmond, and asked me to join him in an expedition that would make us famous and give us plenty of money besides. He has had an interview with several of the leading men of the South, and they have offered him great inducements to prevent the Presidential party—as it is called—fiom ever reaching Washington. He has been entrusted with the carrying out of the whole affair, and I am to join him at the proper time. The plan is fixed and cannot fail. The party must go to Harrisburg. Now between Harrisburg and Washington stands the city of Baltimore. The Gunpowder Bridge is not the safest bridge in the world, if the scheme for operating on it is only properly carried out. But there is danger in that plan that should not be overlooked. The chances are that the trap set to catch the rat—meaning the Presidential party—may only serve to capture a mouse (some other train) and let the rat escape. Thus all our labor and patience would be thrown away; besides, risking the danger of surprising our friends as well as enemies and uselessly destroying life. The South is rich, and would be willing to pay any amount that might be required to secure to them their independence without shedding the blood of her sons; but it does not seem to me likely that she will pay anything at all for a scheme that may end in a total and disgraceful failure. To my mind, it would be as well if Booth and the whole party would talk the matter over again, before deciding on any particular plan. He seems to be impressed with the idea that something can and ought to be done to prevent Lincoln from reaching Washington. I am ready for anything, as he knows, and as I have told him; but still it is my firm opinion that if the independence of the South depends mainly on the fact that Abraham Lincoln is prevented from reaching the city of Washington before the 4th of March, their cause rests upon a very shallow foundation, and a shaky one at that. I do not like a wholesale murder, and would prefer that Lincoln lived, in order that he might be an eye-witness to glorious success of the South in her attempt to obtain her freedom from the tyranny of the Northern Abolitionists.

February 21, 1861.—I saw Booth to-day. Who was that woman he had with him? She seemed to be urging him on against his will. Whenever he failed to speak strongly enough on the subject of to-morrow's work, she at once caught his eye, and he, that bold and daring fellow, quailed as if detected in a crime.

She seems far more resolute than he. But who is she, and what has she to do in the matter? Why did not Booth introduce her by name? There seems to be a strange mystery about all this that should not be between friends and brothers. When he introduced me to the order of the K. G. C., I supposed that there would be no secrets between us, and expected to deal with men, not with women. This matter is of a far too serious character to be trusted to those who would be likely to babble—and women will chatter. I should not be surprised that, by to-morrow night, the ever-present newspaper reporter will have telegraphed, all over the whole South, the plans we have laid out to effect the capture of Lincoln and his party, and we shall have to thank this woman for betraying us—she is bound by neither oath nor obligation. What a fool-hardy trick of Booth to trust such a secret into the hands of a woman. I feel ashamed of my companion.

Washington's Birthday, Morning.—Last night, we met and decided on the plan to be adopted.

The train is to be stopped on Gunpowder Bridge. A number of those roughs who were present at my initiation are then to enter the train, to take possession of the minor characters of the party, and especially to look after the immediate attendants; Rob. is to attend to the reporters, and, being a newspaper man, knows well enough how to keep them all amused; Booth and I are to draw Lincoln and Hamlin out of the car for a minute, when the remainder will be ready to hurry them off to place where they will be safe for some time to come at least.

That is the scheme to be carried out, and cannot well fail. The party sleep at Harrisburg to-night. Booth says that woman is in the secret, having been especially chosen by the Southern Government for the purpose, and that he made her acquaintance in Richmond.

That may all be true, so far as he knows; but I have

no confidence in her. She ought to have known nothing about it. But I can plainly see that Booth is infa-
tuated with that woman ; and, if the impersonation of
Richard has any one failing more than another, it is his
attachment to females and female society. I believe
he would sell his very soul to please a woman with
whom he had become familiarly acquainted. I wonder
where that woman is now. She is not with Booth,
that is certain; for he left me at his hotel and seemed
angry to find she had disappeared.

February 22—Evening.—That woman has returned—
so Booth says—and the plans are all right.

But where has she been all this day? It is very
strange that she should have so suddenly disappeared—
no one knows whither—and has again made herself one
of our party. There is something very strange in all
this, and I like it not. It is my certain opinion that
President Davis, at Montgomery, should never trust
his plans to a woman in Richmond.

I have no faith in women. They are all alike, fickle,
faithless and false. I am convinced that Booth's
woman would sell the whole of us for a twenty-dollar
piece. She looks like it.

But Booth's weak point is woman; and, where she
leads, he is bound to follow. I should have thought
he had seen enough of them by this time to have been
convinced that what I have said to him is true. But
no, he says she is all right, and that her absence has
been from a right motive. Well, if so, I should like
to know that motive, if only to be assured of my own
safety. He believes in her, and may continue so to do;
but I do not, and that is as certain as that I am now
making this entry in my diary.

Should she prove false, I will show this to Booth,
to convince him that the opinion I held of her this
night was what she had proved to be.

Who is she? and why does Booth keep her name so
secret? I do not like women at all! and certainly not

women without names.   There is no good in them, of that I am convinced.

February 23.—Failed !   " Lincoln is in Washington !"   " Went through Baltimore last night in secret."   " The detectives had received notice of a plan to assault, outrage and perhaps assassinate the President while passing through Baltimore."   That 's the heading in this morning's papers.   So all our fine schemes have failed !   But how ?   Who told the detectives ?   I believe, and am convinced that it was no one else but that woman.   I wonder what Booth will say to this paragraph when he sees it.

Booth called on me, and in a rage said, " the bright hope of the Confederacy had faded."   I know that ; and with it all my chances for fame and honor.   Booth seemed like a madman, for he placed more reliance on the effect of this scheme than I ever did.   What good would it have done in the end, by the mere capture and detention of Lincoln ?   And what harm can the States of the South suffer from him, if they are all out of the Union, as they have declared they are ?   Seven states are now out, certain, and the others will follow. From what I know I do not believe that Lincoln is any safer in Washington than he would have been in Baltimore.   If there had been any desire on the part of the order to take his life, that could have been safely accomplished in any of the Northern cities, and as easily as in Baltimore ; and, I am convinced, such a plan, if desired, can yet be accomplished in Washington.   But such a deed is not desired by anyone connected with the welfare of the Southern cause—at least such is my firm opinion.

February 25.—"General Twiggs has surrendered the Army in Texas."   At last the news has reached the North.   How finely the order works out its power. Lincoln is elected, but he is not President of the *United* States.   He is chosen, by the Abolitionists, " Commander-in-Chief of the U. S. Army and Navy," and yet, before he even assumes command, he learns that there is no army to command, and will soon find there is no navy. Had old Scott only been induced to have joined us, there would not have even been a remnant of the Army. The officers are dwindling out one by one; and, even of those that remain, fully one half are bound by oath to support our cause, if any attempt should be made to put down the Seceding States by force.

It is rumored here in Washington that the distant naval squadrons are to be ordered home; but, well I know, that when the vessels come home, there will be no officers to command them. Our friend in the Cabinet have taken care of that, and the Navy is as rotten as the Army. The cause is sacred and secure; and the South can safely defy the whole power of the new Government.

Besides, are not all the offices in the various Bureaus surrounded by our spies, and can anything be done without the South being at once advised by them. The only power in this country, at the present moment, is vested in us, the "Knights of the Golden Circle."

[The next few entries are written in characters, that are entirely unintelligible, except to the initiated.— EDITOR.]

CHAPTER IV.

THE INAUGURATION—FRUSTRATED PLANS.

March 3, 1861.—To-morrow is to be the inauguration; and, in spite of all our preparations, it will take place. What excellent arrangements had been made to have prevented it; and how the whole thing has been spoiled. It is strange that the plans that were made in secret session in Baltimore should have been discovered—at least it appears so by the preparations of the Government. The " Wide Awakes " are to have the place of honor; and it has been impossible to get our members into that order—if order it is. We have not been able to learn any of their secrets, although they appear to know ours. The Headquarters of the K. G. C. has been notified, from New York, that members of the Wide Awake association have been discovered among the " Circles " in that city. Whose fault is that ? There has been too much laxity in the admission of members lately. Desirous of gaining strength, they have admitted candidates who have not been as sound as they ought to have been ; and one rotten plank may perhaps sink a ship. Our meetings are not kept quite secret, and I know the reason of that. To gain the support of certain newspapers, the editors and reporters have been admitted to membership ; and, when it serves their interests, they make money or sensational paragraphs of the most vital points of our secret meetings. Some of these have lately been published in the New York press; and nothing less than treason or treachery could have given those journals the necessary information. I have no faith in newspaper support. It will fail us when we most want it. There are proofs of it at the present time. From the letters that are published in the New York journals, it is plain that spies are traveling through the South. This should have been looked after. Too much information has been given these traveling correspondents. Some of them are moving about with a double character—representing one paper, known to be in our interest, and writing to another. Some of these fellows will yet be hung, as they should be, by the neck or heels, to the first tree near which they may be captured. There should be no mercy shown to traitors. But for treachery, we might at this very hour have been masters of the National Capital; whereas our professed enemies, the Abolitionists, are now in full possession. Our best-laid plans are being defeated. Even in those newspaper offices which are our supporters, are posted the spies of the Abolitionists; and every word uttered within the supposed sacred limits of the Editorial rooms is sent to the Government. I know it. When in the —— office in Baltimore, yesterday, while I was conversing with one of the editors, a Knight, I noticed a man taking notes, in short-hand, of our conversation; and, to-day, one of the clerks in Washington told me that a full report of our conversation had been placed on file in his Bureau. This system of espial will yet defeat us, if measures are not taken to put a stop to it. But how is it to be done?

March 4, 1861.—The inauguration is over. Abraham I, King of Columbia, has been crowned! The plan, agreed upon last night in the Circle here, failed from want of nerve in the party selected to carry it out. But for that, the throne would be vacant. Now will come the hour of trial. The South will not submit to be ruled by an Abolitionist, and the Federal Government will accept of no compromise. Well, we can fight, and we will fight.

I wish Booth would get rid of that woman. I do not like her, and am morally certain she has defeated many of our plans. He places too much confidence in her. She says she is a true daughter of the South; but it is very strange that shortly before any important work is to be done, she disappears for a time, and failure is as certain to be the result. I shall suggest at next meeting that a watch be put upon her movements.

[The daily entries that follow, for the next month, are merely brief records of the progress of events in the South, such as: "*March* 6, Fort Brown surrendered." &c., and therefore only useful to the sta-

tistical reader. They are therefore omitted here.—
EDITOR.]

April 5, 1861.—It is very plain that the South has
not looked forward quite as wisely as they might have
done. Why did they not secure Fort Sumter in the
same way that the other defences had been taken care
of? Have they been deceived in Anderson? Did
they think that because he was a Southern man, he was
certain to be in sympathy with our cause? If so, the
policy was short-sighted, to say the least of it. They
ought to have taken warning by New York City, in
which were to be found a number of Northern men,
(members of our own order,) who have no sympathy
with the Northern cause. Sumter will cause us
trouble yet. Anderson says he will not give it up, and
while he remains there, his position is a menace both
to Moultrie and the city of Charleston. But will he
dare to fire on the South? Yes, I believe he will dare
anything, if he is driven to it. And yet it will not be
wise to allow the Federal flag to wave at the entrance
to the harbor; and thus show to the world that we
have no power to pull it down. South Carolina is
making preparations to bombard the Fort; but whether
she will do it, remains to be seen. She was the first
to inaugurate secession—will she be the first to open a
war? And if a war is commenced—will Lincoln re-
taliate by making war on the South? Should he declare war, will the Northern States respond? We are
sure of the Governors of Virginia, Kentucky and Mis-
souri—they belong to us—but the Northern States
have all chosen Abolitionists, who would only be too
glad of the chance of fighting the South for their
darling theory. War seems to be certain; but yet we
have a strong influence in the North that may be
brought to bear on the minds of the people. Some of
the militia are sworn to us, and they will either refuse
to go, or disband and join our forces. The cause is
far from lost. and Fort Sumter will be the test.

April 6, 1861.—Have just seen one of us in the Navy Department. He says a vessel is under orders to sail with troops, arms and provisions from New York for Fort Sumter.

Have consulted with some of the Circle, and it is agreed to send on a cypher dispatch to give warning of the movement.

Dispatch sent this evening.

April 7, 1861.—The steamer has started with the troops—at least my informant has so stated—but she will never get to Fort Sumter.

April 8, 1861.—The Government has notified the Governor of South Carolina that Fort Sumter shall be re-inforced—by force, if necessary. Too late, they know it already.

Booth's woman tried to find out from me what were to be our plans in the event of a war breaking out. I am not quite so easily to be worked upon as Booth, so she ascertained—nothing.

The Abolitionists would not receive the Confederate Commissioners, on the ground that " Government cannot form treaties with subjects." King Abraham I. will find but few Americans that will acknowledge themselves to be his subjects. What a fine theme to work upon the minds of the Northerners. I shall move that matter to-night in the Circle, and see if we cannot make the answer a first-rate lever to work upon.

Two more steamers directed to sail from New York for the South, under sealed orders. Where to? Charleston, I suppose. They know it by this time, and will give the invaders a warm reception.

April 9, 1861.—The preparations are all complete at Charleston, and the Fort is to be bombarded. Our work meanwhile is to raise up sympathy in the North for the Confederates, and to declare that Anderson will only make a show of fighting, and then surrender. Leave to-night for other places in which I can operate better, as troops are arriving here under a pretense of defending the capital. Spies are about everywhere; but we have received ample warning.

April 12, 1861.—Arrived here (N. Y.) last night. Have been busily at work in Baltimore, Philadelphia and Trenton. The order is doing well everywhere.

The fighting has commenced at Charleston. Anderson is said to be really fighting in earnest; but we are encouraging our friends by the statements that it is only a mere feint, and that the shots are so aimed that they will not hurt anyone. Lincoln said that there is "nobody hurt," and of course we have repeated his words with good effect. The North is greatly divided.

April 13, 1861.—Great excitement here (N. Y.) about the fighting; but everybody appears to wish the South will win. The papers are issuing extras with all the dispatches received from the South. The *Herald* supports our cause bravely.

April 14, 1861.—The News has reached New-York that the United States flag has been lowered from over Sumter. Great excitemen there. (N. Y.) The feeling of the people seems to be changing, and, if it lasts, there will be a fearful war. Our work very difficult.

April 15, 1861.—Rode about in the cars, and tried to advocate the cause of the South. Was more than once threatened with personal violence. The excitement is terrible. Must wait until it subsides.

April 16, 1861.—The *Herald* out for us strongly. People very excited, and demanded of the *Herald* that it should show its colors. Had no colors to show, and borrowed a flag from a neighboring flag-maker. Called on them to know the reason of such a display of buntine, and was referred to the Chief Editor, who was not to be seen.

Lincoln calls out the militia. Some of the regiments are responding, and the people are urging them on. Unless the feeling changes, this is no place for me.

Several of the Knights have been subjected to personal violence.

April 17, 1861.—The *Herald* against us to-day ; as strongly in favor of the Government, as it was against it yesterday.   The excitement is so great that we cannot work, and must leave for a better field.

Left for Philadelphia, and found the field of operations there no better to work upon than in New-York. Tried my best, in company with others, and got knocked down twice.   Determined to return to Baltimore.

April 18, 1861.—Arrived this morning in Baltimore. Great excitement everywhere. Met Booth here. He had been to Montgomery, which is chosen as the Confederate provisional capital.   He had been playing there as a "star," and had succeeded better than might have been expected.   His former experience on the stage might have led him to expect a different result; but, in my opinion, success arose more from his connection with our order than from any extra display of genius. He had given out here in Baltimore that his reason for returning North, is in consequence of an injury he had met with from the accidental explosion of a pistol ; but, in private, I learned that he had been chosen as a secret agent to visit the North and inflame the minds of the doubtful, strengthen those who remained favorable to the cause, and counteract against the influences of the Abolitionists, who have begun to gain an unusual ascendancy over the minds of the people.   He has invited me to join him in the work.

Met in secret conclave with the Knights, to consult as to the best means to be adopted to prevent the troops from reaching the National Capital.   Remained in session late tonight, and finally resolved on our plans, which were very systematically laid out—having been assisted at our consultations by some advice from able military officers, now on duty in Washington, and who have been used to campaigning.   The signal agreed upon, for the commencement of operations, is to be the arrival of the Northern troops—and we shall learn of their approach through our friends in the telegraph office—and further assistance will be afforded by the non-interference of Kane's police. This will give us a better opportunity to locate our various operating parties.

Now the work begins in earnest. Success must and will attend us.

CHAPTER V.

THE EXCITEMENT IN BALTIMORE—ATTACK ON THE TROOPS.

April 19, 1861, *Morning*—Well, we have our work before us, and I trust there will be no failure this time. From all the preparation, and from the well-known feelings of those residing in the city of Baltimore, the prospects are everything that could be desired.

What a meeting took place here on the night of the 17th. It is really surprising that such assemblies should have been allowed; but, then, the police are all on our side, and, that being the case, there is no one to say—that care to say anything that would be likely to have any effect upon the matter—that is, so far as it would influence the stopping of the public assemblies. As long as they cannot bring a charge against the supporters of the South, of having committed an overt act against the peace of the country, these meetings will doubtless go on; and every one knows well that, in spite of both President and political partizanship, they will have their influence on the masses farther north.

So far as Baltimore is concerned, the reduction of the Fort in Charleston Harbor has done us no harm.

It is only in the cities farther north that it has proved an evil; and now that the troops are on the move, the mercurial feelings of the people have reached a high point—blood heat. But this will soon subside, and then we must to work again.

The fall of Sumter has certainly gained us a number of friends here, at any rate. The "demonstration meeting," as it is called, was certainly one of the most excited of its kind, and, as far as sentiment was concerned, was equal to any thing that the best friends of the South could have desired. What fiery speeches!— that is, if any reliance can be placed on the reports that appeared in the papers here. I thought, and have been told, that Booth is a good actor on the stage; but he never could have excelled, even in his favorite character of Richard III., the great speech made by him at that meeting. All the city is full of it, and every second man is praising him for what he then said. Well! he loves fame, and he has it now, at any rate.

I was expected, by some of our party, to have been in the city on the 17th, and to have delivered a speech to the meeting. It is said that my name was set down by the committee to have said something startling to the people. But then I do not waste time in talking—I act. Even had I been here, it would have been next to useless to have attempted to have followed Booth in a speech suitable to the occasion. I might, with just as many chances for success, have tried to have put my arms around the monument in the Square, for the purpose of leveling it with the earth, as to have thought of following Booth in a speech upon such a subject. Besides which, I was elsewhere employed, and otherwise engaged.

What an excitable fellow Booth is! Ambitious for fame, he sometimes allows himself to be carried away beyond his fair reason. For instance (and I shall here record it for future reference) as we were coming away from the Circle last night, he and I had some conversation on the character of the excitement and feeling of the people in the city of New York.

"What," asked he, with very evident anxiety," are the chances of a change?"

"None," I answered, promptly.

"None!" he repeated, somewhat savagely. "And pray why do you say that word so positively?"

"Because I have had a chance of knowing," I replied.

"Where are the Knights?" asked he.

"They have not the slightest chance to act there," was my answer; "with any degree of safety."

"Safety!" repeated he. "Are they cowards?"

The tone of contempt and derision with which these three words were uttered, plainly showed to my mind the character of the man, with whom I was thus brought in contact. He seemed to think that the names of Knight of the Golden Circle and coward, could not be spoken with the same breath.

Wishing to check his anger a little, I answered with a plain but simple

"No!"

"Then why," he inquired, "are they afraid to face a little feeling of temporary excitement, which may subside in a few hours? Have they forgotten that the cause of the South is both a righteous and just cause— men rising for the support and maintenance of their priceless liberty?"

To this I replied in words indicating that the uprising in New York was no more spontaneous ebullition of party feeling, but the kindling of an enthusiastic patriotism, mingled with fanaticism. This feeling, I informed him, was so great in the metropolis, that the first word uttered in a public place in support of the South, was sure to be followed by a severe blow from some person present.

Booth knitted his brows and ground his teeth with some amount of savageness in his manner.

"Such knock-down arguments," I added, "cannot be considered as pleasant, or the best means to be employed to keep up a man's courage. I don't mind a blow when there is a fair chance of retaliating; but to be sent to earth, amid the jeers of those who are not in sympathy with you, and to hear the shout of 'serve him right' ringing in your ears as you fall, is not exactly pleasant. Beside which, when you are down, there is not a single person in the city who would 'step out of his way to help you up, or even to defend you from assaults while rising to your feet."

Again Booth ground his teeth as if with a kind of impotent rage, and glared at me with the look of a tiger deprived of his prey.

"Their time will yet come" said he.

Before I could reply he looked up with a different expression of countenance—his face being overspread with a curiously sardonic smile—and he muttered a few quotations from his favorite author, Shakspeare. The selections were taken from his principal characters, and seemed to apply as well to the actual state of affairs as if he had written them to suit the time and occasion.

After a while he resumed the conversation in a more natural mood and tone of voice.

"So, so," he remarked, "the North, or rather the so-called pro-slavery democrats of the North, are not to be relied on in this crisis?"

I replied in the negative.

"And those who have fattened on the South," he continued, "and who have promised us their full support, when required—have they now turned their backs upon us?"

My reply was simply an unqualified affirmative.

"And this will apply to the whole North?" asked he, in a sharp, quick tone.

"In this," I replied, "the North is a unit."

"Then may the eternal gods wither them!" he ejaculated through his set teeth; "and, if they hope to subdue the South, may their desires be turned into ashes, that shall scatter and eat into their own flesh."

" Amen" I responded.

Booth now relapsed into a sullen silence, of a very moody character ; and as I had no desire to be treated to any more dramatic exhibitions, nor felt in any mood to listen to his theatrical outpourings of venom, I also kept silent on the subject, and we walked home together to his hotel. I noticed, however, that he appeared to walk still very lame, from his recent accident at Montgomery.

I called this morning on the Chief of police, and have received assurances that everything has been done that can be done to render our work this morning easy. Of course, he will not appear to act in the matter, as all our movements are supposed to be unknown to him.

During the early hours, both Booth and I have been moving about among the roughs, and, where I found the love of riot was not a sufficient inducement to make them join us in the coming movement, I worked upon their love of State.

"If," I intimated, " if Maryland would secure for herself that independence she most desires—to make her own laws and govern her own citizens—she must herself strike the blow for freedom. Remember" I added, "the men who would now oppose the South are Yankee abolitionists, who have no soul above the price of a dollar, and would swap away the very jack-knife that may be required in the day's work."

These remarks did more to inflame the passions of those men than all the offers of money or the temptations of plunder, and I feel sure of their support at the right moment. I——.

[Here the diary appears to end somewhat abruptly, as if the writer had been disturbed at the moment of commencing a sentence, and doubtless, judging from the contexts, it was the anxiously expected arrival of troops that had caused him to break off in his entries— Editor.]

April 19, 1861. *Evening*—Well, the day is over, and all the city is in a perfect furore of excitement. We have been entirely successful; and the first victory on the soil north of the Potomac has been achieved by the South, to-day, in the city of Baltimore. Those who sympathise with us are masters of the city to-night.

This is the anniversary of the battle of Lexington, and I look upon this fact as a good omen for the future. The South must win the day in the end; and, if they only act as promptly as we have done, great news will reach us soon from our neigboring city of Washington. I trust the Sons of the Old Dominion have not been behind-hand in their movements, and have followed up promptly what we have so ably begun.

Although the motive power, that has assisted in driving on the mighty machine, Booth and I, like the hidden steam, have as yet taken no outwardly active part in the affair of to-day. We have given the orders, and they are sure to be ably carried out, by others less likely to be recognized by-and-by.

Our plans have been completely successful, and the few troops that have passed through the city, have not escaped without carrying the marks of war with them. They came to make war upon the South, and South-erners have administered the first blow, both here and in Charleston.

Never were plans so ably made, so skillfully concoct-ed, and so excellently carried out. The operations have been executed at the same time on all sides. No more Yankee troops will ever pass through the city of Baltimore for the purpose of invading the Southern States of this Republic—or rather the States of the New Republic. Perhaps the Yankees will remember this day for some time, and leave us alone—that is all we ask.

Booth and I have had the principal management of the whole affair, although neither of us have appeared on the scene of strife. This precaution will render us less objects of suspicion from meddlesome persons; and we will be able to operate better in this quiet way, than if we were better known.

For once in his lifetime, Booth has been able to carry out a project without the advice or assistance of a woman. Queen Anne was Richard's bane, and had that creature of John's but been aware of what our operations were to have been, ten to one they would have been spoiled. As it is, all has gone off as well as could have been desired.

We have taken every one by surprise—North, South and Centre. Even the authorities—those who were in the secret—are amazed at the amount of our success. It is no ordinary success. All the railroads leading in and through this city have been destroyed—either broken up, cut down or burned. Not a single Yankee soldier can be sent from the North through Baltimore to Washington, and they cannot reach that city by any other route. Neither can the Abolitionists in the Capital send troops north to suppress this movement here. The road from Annapolis to Washington is also thoroughly torn up by this time, therefore the Abolitionists cannot reach the city where Abraham I. reigns, even by vessels from the South. The Potomac is also guarded at points that will prevent troops from ascending that river; and the City of Magnificent Distances is cut off from its "loving people." Lincoln and his crew will be starved out, as they have a couple of thousand more than ordinary to feed.

The telegraphs have also been cut in every direction, therefore information of our movements cannot well be sent on in either direction. This will prevent the concentration of troops for some time, and as delays are sometimes of great value in gigantic struggles, something may be gained by this.

Virginia has declared herself for the Confederacy,
and now she will have to fight for it as well. If
her sons have only been ready to act, Washington
ought by this time to be in the hands of those who
are favorable to the cause of the Independence of the
Southern States as a separate Confederacy from the
Northern.

[The entries that follow for the next few days show
plainly that a disreputable state of anarchy reigned
within the city of Baltimore, and that the writer and
Booth were intimately mixed up with the whole affair.
As these facts are matters of history, and are of too
great a length to be embodied in this small work, it
has deemed advisable to omit their publication in this
edition.—EDITOR.]

CHAPTER VI.

SURRATT'S RELATIONS WITH NORTHERN MERCHANTS.

May 15, 1861.—Visited New York yesterday, having escaped the surveillance of the military forces now
stationed in Baltimore.

That city is becoming somewhat dangerous, just
now, for the members of our order to act therein; and
the military commander, which the Abolitionist President has chosen to place over a free people, is a perfect
tyrant. "Set a thief to catch a thief" is an old max-
im, and a true one; therefore place a turncoat democrat
in power over democrats and he is their bitterest
enemy. The citizens of Baltimore will yet find out
what a tyrant they have had placed over them. Not
a movement is made without his knowledge; and in a
short time, the poor unfortunate Southern patriot finds
himself in the grasp of the military power. Thus is

the Constitution overridden by petty tyrants, and the true born sons of the South are held down by their Yankee oppressors. They will soon, if they can, make slaves of every white man of the South, and none will be so ready to aid in such a measure as that Yankee lawyer turned soldier.

Called to-day on the large shipping firm of———* to whom I had letters of introduction. They are in the " Circle" and have contracted to supply the South with a large quantity of arms, uniforms, stores, &c. The letter, together with our private means of introduction, has made me receive a very friendly welcome, and by their instrumentality I hope to be able to move among some very influential persons in the North so as to carry out my mission of sowing discussion among the ranks of the Abolitionists. If it is only possible to retard the enlistment *furore*, perhaps some little advantage may be gained thereby.

By-the-way, it seems very strange to me that this firm can take a large order from the Yankee President to supply the troops of the North with uniforms, and yet will contract with the South for the same purpose. I spoke to———,the leading partner, on 'the subject and he says, the taking of the orders by him from the State Authorities of the North, is a blind to cover up the others.

"If uniforms were to leave here, without such a precaution, it would bring upon us the vigilance of the Police, who have been invested with a sort of semi-military authority. Had the old fashioned Mayor's Police been in existence, we should have been all right; for those, who would then have been in command, would have done all they could to have served the cause of the South and retard the operations of the North."

---

* As it may affect the administration of justice, the name of this firm, which is now in existence, has been omitted ; but will doubtless appear in subsequent editions.—EDITOR.

" But how can you supply both ?" asked I.

" Easily enough," replied the merchant. " When I want to send a large quantity of uniforms South, they are made up into bales with a Federal uniform on the outside edges. They are then directed to Washington, by a certain route, and put on board the steamer. Should the steamer by chance stop at Norfolk, or be delayed along the coast in that vicinity, or off the point off Maryland, that is not our fault ; and there, why, it is probable, the vessel might be boarded from some boat from the South sent out from the shore. Such being the case, the uniforms would be seized as contraband of war and landed—we taking care that no resistance is offered to the boarders by the officers or crew of the vessel. Even if the articles be thus seized, we do not lose any thing as you are doubtless aware. It would be impossible for the whole coast to be so guarded as to prevent us thus landing the cargo ; and no suspicion can possibly fall upon us in the transaction."

I, at once, praised the scheme, when he added,

" You therefore perceive that it would be impossible to execute such a plan unless we took a contract from the North ; or, under that, *and our untarnished reputation*, we are enabled to carry out our contract with the South, in the manner I have just explained."

" But what could the South do with the Federal uniforms," I asked, innocently.

" Clothe their spies," answered the merchant, with a smile at my want of acuteness.

" Suppose, now," I remarked, " that Lincoln's myrmidons should find this out, what would be the result of the affair ?"

" Such result is beyond supposition," he answered. " Our loyalty is too well established to admit of doubt. Are not our names down on the subscription list of the Chamber of Commerce for a large sum to carry on the

War against the South ; therefore could we be supposed for one moment to aid them. No, sir," he added, with a self-complacent smile," we could deny all knowledge of the goods, and our word would be quite sufficient."

"Did you subscribe to that list the other day ?" I asked, in a tone that betrayed my great surprise.

"Certainly," he replied ; "why not. I have made more than the amount in profits already on my contracts, North and South ; and before the war is ended —for a war will surely be the result of this affair— I shall have found the investment to have been a good one."

"But will the South agree to it ?" I asked, quietly.

"What will they care ?" he answered, interrogatively ; " provided they get their supplies, and I can retard the delivery of those for the North."

"How do you inform the South when goods are on any of your steamers for them ?" was my next question.

"If you ask direct questions, young man," said the Senior partner, " we must refuse to answer you, even in spite of your credentials. Suffice it to say, they know when the goods are on hand, and look out accordingly. Not one single bale of Southern goods has ever yet gone astray ; although several of those belonging to the Northern troops have fallen into the hands of our friends. I have a large order now in the house, only waiting shipment, and this will be done to-day."

Satisfied on this score I broke up the conversation— as it seemed evident that they were desirous of saying as little as possible—by presenting a draft upon them from one of the provisional officers of the Confederate Government. It was, without hesitation, instantly honored in gold ; although specie payments had been stopped at the banks for some time.

"I have given you gold, sir," said the merchant, "because all our transactions with the South are on a gold basis."

From further conversation which I had with these gentlemen, I learned that a large amount of gold is lying at the present time in England, subject to the drafts of New York contractors, and that all merchants, doing an illicit trade with the South, would be able to rest assured of payment for the goods they might supply—the presentation of the bill of lading, to the Confederate agent resident in New York, being sufficient evidence of the completion of the order—the South taking all risks of safe carriage and delivery.

By this information I became convinced that the the South have well arranged their plans for the carrying on of a war—if such is to be found necessary—and that they had been attending to such matters for a long time. I had, some time since, found out how they had managed to sow discord among the people of the North; but little suspected they had taken such precautions as these. The North is far from being prepared for such a struggle, for the very men they trust will deceive them; but the South has reliable agents everywhere, both in the Northern States and in Europe.

Have not seen Booth for some days, nor that woman of his. It seems to me likely they have gone South. Perhaps I might do better to remain here, and shall certainly do as long as it pays.

[Here follows a calculation of figures, as if the writer had suddenly thought that the accounts between him and the South were not exactly squared up; for, upon comparing the descriptions of the items of expenses with the foregoing diary, it is evident that the figures related, to some extent, to his movements for the Southern cause. Should this really be the case, John H. Surratt must have been in the habit of drawing a princely fortune, as an income, for his expenditure

was of the most lavish character up to this date.   Th
list of names from whom he has apparently draw
largely, is also very interesting; as it shows that
number of prominent merchants in New-York wer
acting as agents for the Southern Confederacy durin;
the first year of the war.

The subsequent entries during the month of Ma)
with the exception of the allusion to Ellsworth's deatl
and also those for the first ten days of June, are of n
interest to the reader, as they relate principally t
family matters, and trivial events of his private life
The only value of these items is, to establish th
genuineness of the whole document, as many of th
matters, therein entered, are such as only one keepin;
a diary for his own personal convenience would be lik
to record.   He alludes to remittances sent to hi
mother at different times, but gives no account of th
purposes to which the sums thus sent were to be ap
plied.   The items for traveling expenses, entered a
different times, shew that he must have been movin;
about a great deal; and the occasional entries o
"Called on F. W.," "Visited J. K.," "Presented lette
to H. S.," and so on, indicate that he was not merel)
traveling for pleasure.   Perhaps these initials may ye
be explained, when the parties concerned will doubt
less be exposed, if they deserve exposure.

It is rather unfortunate, for the contiuity of thi;
diary, that the writer has omitted to name the places
from which he dates his entries; otherwise they migh
serve as a clue to guide a sharp detective to identify
the numerous persons mentioned only by. initials.
Even, as it is, there is but little doubt the Government
prosecutor has, and still will use his best endeavors to
find out the persons alluded to—if only to obtan thei
evidence in such matters as may give the slightest clue
to the connection of the assassins with the late Rebel
Government.   It may be, however, that those names
that are given plainly will suffice.—EDITOR.]

CHAPTER VII.

CURIOUS MATTERS CONCERNING THE EARLY BATTLES.

June 12, 1861.—So the Yankees have been beaten in the first battle on Virginian soil. This might have been expected by them if they had only taken the matter into proper consideration.

The South is fully prepared for War, and have best officers in the country ; while the North is both without officers, men or military education. If the South can only prevent the Yankees from advancing along upon Southern soil, there is no doubt but that France and England will recognize the Confederacy. One thing is certain the Yankees will not soon forget their reception at Big Bethel.

June 15, 1861.—Ascertained to-day from M. W., at the War Department, that a movement is to be made upon Richmond very soon by way of Centerville and Manasses. The plan of operations has been submitted and is on file. He has provided me a copy of the plan ; and, if I get it, must manage in some way to forward or take it to Richmond.

June 17, 1861.—Have received a copy of the proposed plan and shall start to-morrow for Richmond.

Drew on R. F. for the necessary expenses.

[A vacancy here takes place in the entries, as if the writer had placed his diary in some place of concealment, while making his intended trip to Richmond.—EDITOR.]

June 26, 1861.—Not quite so easy to get to Richmond as in former times. What with military guards at different points along the coast, the gunboats patrolling the river, and the Confederate sharpshooters on the Virginia banks of the Potomac, I have run through such a gauntlet, as would have required almost a charmed life to have succeeded in escaping all the dangers. But I am pretty well acquainted with al the by-paths, nooks and creeks of Lower Marylan(and the Eastern Shore, and in spite of Military law, an(sentinels. I have managed pretty well to get back saf(to Surrattsville.

It required a little ingenuity to get to the coast with out exciting the suspicions of the guard stationed alon(the road; but persons on such business as mine rarel follow traveled roads. But then, the K. G C. has; fine network of connections along to the Point; an(when the road was considered to be dangerous, I re ceived full warning in time.

By employing a few good, reliable agents, I manage(to have fishing boats laying up the creeks on mor(than one point of the coast, so that, when compelle(to forsake one of the proposed places of embarkation I had others to which I could resort. Twice I narrow ly escaped capture from a sentinel having been but re cently located at a place that I had considered open but, by good luck, the dangers were in both case avoided tn time.

Having got safely on board the boat, two attempt; were made to cross the river after sunset; but th(brightness of the moon made everything on the rive so clearly visible, that, had we pushed far into th(stream, we should certainly have been discovere(by those confounded patrol boats, or river police as it i; called.

Three nights since, we were favored with a murk; sky, and this induced an attempt to cross the river The moon had not risen when we started, and all alon(the "Silver Potomac" a deathlike stillness reigned, dis turbed only by the sound of distant paddle wheels o the patrol boats.

The darkness was favorable in one thing, but un favorable in another; for we could not see which wa; to steer our little vessel. We were fearful of runnin(against the police steamers, or Potomac flotilla, whicl might be lying at anchor in the stream; and this would certainly have resulted in my capture. We might also, by the variation of a point, make our way out sea, instead of across to Virginia; and this would have produced no very pleasing result. And if we got safely across, as it was too murky to see a signal, we stood a chance of being fired upon by our friends in the batteries; and, perhaps, a stray shot might pick us off. Danger everywhere.

"Those who would pass here, must face both fire and steel."

I had not forgotten those important words, and was, of course, ready to do so; and, therefore, gave the order to push across at any risk.

When we reached about the midway of the river, the rising moon began to whiten the clouds, causing a kind of twilight, more confusing than darkness. We could see nothing ten yards beyond the head of the boat. Still we pushed on, and soon began to perceive by the soundings that we were nearing the shore.

A flash, followed by a report, was the next thing observable; but whether from the shore or police boat we could not then determine. This want of knowledge prevented me from showing my signal light, and the next minute, another flash, report, and something heavy dropped into the water, not far from where we were.

"Too good an aim," thought I, "to be either pleasant or agreeable."

The rowers in the boat, having no such inducements as I had to risk their lives, began to grumble about the danger they were running and wished to turn back. I endeavored to show them that there was as much danger in going backward as forward; but they did not seem to approve of my logic.

A third flash, report and a bouncing object in the water next ensued; and, almost before the sound passed away, a flash appeared behind us, followed also by a shot and report. We were between two fires, and the danger was imminent.

Securing my papers, so as to be ready to throw them at any moment into the river, I determined to risk the chances and display my signal light in the direction whence the first gun was fired. In a moment the light flashed over the water in the manner agreed upon between the order both North and South. An answer was quickly returned; but, through the mist, it was only discernable by the peculiar motion made by the light, and not by its color.

The signals had not been seen by the vessel in the river—at least we judged so by the fact that no more shots were fired from behind us; but we heard the sound of paddlewheels, as if the captain of the steamer was resolved to risk the venture of running ashore, in the hope of effecting our capture—for we had no doubt but that our design in crossing the river was more than we suspected.

We could plainly hear the rattle of the wheels, as the steamer drew nearer, and I urged the rowers to use their endeavors in the attempt to gain the shore as speedily as possible. They answered only by a renewal of their utmost exertions.

It was now on our part a race for life and liberty, with the dread of death and capture; while honor and perhaps, as they believed, prize money, offered a strong inducement to the officers and men of the steamer.

We could hear that the steam on the vessel had been increased, as the revolutions of the wheels were plainly more rapid each time.

"Row quicker, boys." I replied, "It is either the shore or a prison for all of us."

" You'se jes right, mass', " replied one of them, "and dat's what dis chile tort all 'long."

Quicker and still quicker flew the boat across the water; but we could hear that the steamer was gaining on us. It was a question of very close calculation whether the strong arms of the rowers would, by their exertions, enable our little bark to outstrip the steam-propelled, yet bulky steamer, or not.

"Row, boys, row faster," said I, anxiously. "A twenty-dollar gold piece to each of you if we escape the steamer."

The offer of reward, and fear of capture, made the rowers still further increase their exertions, and in about five minutes I was pleased to hear the keel of the boat grating along the beach. We were ashore.

Without stopping to consider where I should alight I sprang from the boat, fortunately on dry land, and the next moment was saluted by a sentry with the usual cry of

"Who goes there?"

My reply was promptly given, and an officer was sent for, who happened to be acquainted with the signs agreed upon between the Knights. He was one of us.

In a few moments a flash and report came from the battery near by, and a shot made its way across the water in the direction of the sound of the approaching wheels. A rattling reply followed, and a number of musket balls flew around us, but without causing any injury to either of the party present.

The two rowers rushed up the bank, in perfect fright and terror; but in spite of this, they did not forget to ask for the twenty-dollar gold pieces I had promised them, and which they of course received.

An engagement then ensued between the battery and the steamer, and, finding it safer to be out of range, I withdrew from the line of fire, and prepared to make my way to the Capital, at Richmond, where I expected to meet with a good welcome.

The means was provided for me to reach Fredericksburg, at which point I was enabled to get upon the cars, bound for the city of Richmond, the Capital of the Confederate States.

[The diary does not give any account of what transpired during this visit, nor with whom the interview was held; neither does it state by what means he regained the Maryland shore. From this silence it may easily be supposed that but little danger was experienced in recrossing, and that he returned by the same route. The Records of the Rebellion mention an engagement about this time between a Confederate Battery and U. S. Steamer near the the Rappahannock river, and this was doubtless the very engagement thus alluded to by John H. Surratt.—EDITOR.]

CHAPTER VIII.

THE "BULL RUN" PANIC EXPLAINED.

July 21, 1861, *Midnight.*—So the vaunted boasts of the Yankees have proved to be mere empty brag. The advance movement is checked—that is, the Yankee Army that was to have marched triumphantly "on to Richmond," have discovered that Washington is a far safer place. The followers of the Patriarch have found a Jordan that is not so easily crossed as in the time of Moses. The children of Abraham could find no Joshua to lead them to a promised land. What with the information General Beauregard had received of the proposed movements, and the success of our plans in creating a panic among the Yankees, it is no wonder that the South gained the day.

How finely has the order spread its members among the ranks of the Yankee army, fastened itself on the staffs of leading officers, obtained various commands in the different divisions, from the field officer to the simple corporal, and so have been able to spread dismay throughout the whole army. So well have they managed to excite alarm among the men, that the simple mention of a "masked battery" will make a Yankee's hair stand on end; and the cry of the "Black Horse Cavalry are coming," will make a regiment run.

It was no easy task to work upon the feelings of these Yankee soldiers, and has required weeks of cautious and incessant labor to accomplish it. But when the proper amount of dread was instilled into their minds, the slightest word of alarm was enough to effect the whole of the fighting forces.

By the skillful agency of Captain M——, one of the best fighting regiments was put into disorder, and then, when the cry of "the Black Horse Cavalry are coming" was raised, they fled like sheep—he declaring, as the men were making their way back at a quicker rate than "double,"

"The South deserve their independence, for they won it bravely."

Through the agency of one of the order, holding a high position in the War Department, the chief commands were given to our sworn friends; and, as a natural consequence, when they could have easily won the day, a movement purposely misdirected, an order not understood and therefore disobeyed, and a retreat ordered at a moment when by an advance a victory might have been gained, secured the triumph for the South. Colonel D—— M—— might have done a great deal to prevent the panic of to-day; but then he knew it would not be for our interest. And when he failed to give the proper support at the exact time of its usefulness, those who had borne the worst part of the struggle began to despair of success, and became panic-stricken. The consequence is, that the Yankee army is now a broken mass, or rather a mob; and should the brave boys of the South only advance to-night on this city of Washington, they would find no material obstacle in the way of making an easy capture. But if they neglect this opportunity, they will never get another.

How well the rumor was circulated that Winchester was impregnably fortified, thus causing the officers of the "left wing"—as it is called—of the army to refrain from making an attack. Such is the dread now felt of batteries—both masked and plain—that not one single regiment would dare to advance upon them. So well do I believe has the feeling of alarm been spread abroad, that the troops now forming the Northern army will never again take the field.

July 22, 1862.—The whole army is back, under the protection of the defences of Washingtom, and many of the regiments are without an organization. The whole force is demoralized, and would not make an hour's stand against the advance of a good army. I have already sent a pigeon off with the news, but the chances are that before the Confederates make a forward movement, the *morale*—a fine word of Scott's—of the Yankees will be restored.

I have just heard that the militia forces are to be sent back to their various homes, and their places supplied by regularly enlisted volunteer troops, who are to be properly trained, before any other forward movement is to be made. This will take a long time, and now I must proceed to work, to help the Knights with their new employment—that of preventing and retarding, as much as possible, the enlistment of these three-year volunteers.

Received to-day a notification, from the Central Headquarters of the K. C. G., to endeavor when possible to obtain commissions for Knights in the newly organized regiments of volunteers. The circular has this clause, which I think valuable enough to transcribe for future reference:

"If we can do nothing else, our influence should be

so brought to bear, upon such official authorities within reach, that shall secure, when possible, the appointment of such officers to the command of regiments as shall be beneficial instead of detrimental to our interests."

July 23, 1861.—The enlistment *furore* greater than ever; but to some extent hindered by the concerted action of the Knights, whose slight words of encouragement have been so artfully uttered that, while appearing to favor the movement and support the efforts of the Federal Government to obtain volunteers, have really caused many who were ready and anxious to join the army to re-consider their action, and in several cases to withdraw altogether. In New York City, Philadelphia and Boston, this plan has worked with great perfection; but caution is required here, in consequence of the existence and exercise of Martial Law.

July 25, 1851.—Met to-day in Pennsylvania Avenue, two noted politicians of New York, well known to have publicly favored the cause of the South, and who have recently been appointed colonels of New York regiments. They not only belong to us, but have informed me that every officer under them is a member of the K. G. C. Of course, they do not intend to fight against the South; only entered the military service to divert suspicion from their former actions; and intend, on the first opportunity, when their commands shall be ordered to the front, to give to the Confederates all the information of plans, movements, &c., that may be beneficial to the Southern cause.

" If," said one of them to me, " any of our commands should desert to the enemy, it would be very difficult to prevent it on a dark night."

" Yes," added the other, less cautious, from the fact that law had not been so much practised by him, except in breach, " and if the whole regiment should suddenly resolve to march over, armed and equipped, to the South, how could we prevent it?"

As I listened to them, I thought that James and John were great disciples, and would readily follow the divine instructions of their Master.

[The diary here becomes very explicit with regard to the names of several who held important commands in the army, and who were connected with the K. G. C. On reference to the Army Registers of the States and Regular Service, it appears that many of these very officers were either tried by Court Martial and disgraced, or were dismissed the service without trial. Want of space prevents the publication of the names in this edition.—EDITOR.]

CHAPTER IX.

THE ELECTION OF 1862.

[During the remainder of the year 1861, and the first ten months of 1862, but little matter of general interest is entered in the Diary, with the exception of his record of leaving college, and the sensation he there caused at the time; allusions to the movements of troops, and engagements of the contending forces; comments upon the feelings of the people; the preliminary proclamation for setting all the slaves in the South free, &c., &c. Entries under different dates show how the K. G. C. were operating in order to secure the nomination of members to the various State offices throughout the North, and each success is duly recorded. Had the Diary but been discovered during the existence of the Rebellion and of Martial Law, there is but little doubt that several persons, who now enjoy their liberty with honor, would have been inmates of the military prisons throughout the country.

This discovery might have saved the lives of many brave men, who fell on the field of battle, and would have perhaps prevented the fearful deed for which the criminal is now about to be tried; but the believers in destiny would, perhaps, assert that it was never intended that the book should be brought to light until some great work had been accomplished. What that work was, or has been, is for them to decide, not for the editor of this volume.

Whenever it has been considered best to leave out any of the entries, it has been done wholly with the view to save space in this little volume, not with the intention of shielding any one from public censure. The Courts of Justice will doubtless have all the facts made known in due time, even should it not be considered judicious to publish the Diary complete with all its details.—EDITOR.]

November 1, 1862.—We may consider ourselves sure of the elections in the North this time, thanks to the perseverence of our friends; but the recent pretended exposures of our body is having a damaging effect, and placing people on their guard against strangers. The order of the Government, making it a punishable offence to discourage enlistments, interferes seriously with our operations with the volunteers. We have, however succeeded in changing the furious war feeling of the Americans themselves, and now the Government has to resort to foreign countries to help to fill up their required quotas of troops. If we can but secure the elections this month, we may be sure that no very strong efforts will be made by the individual States to supply the troops; and then look out for trouble in the North.

November 4, 1862.—Victory! A greater one than all the battles that have been fought. The elections have all gone in favor of the Southern party. The people are tired of the war, and are crying out for peace. Some of the newly-elected Governors, especially ——, are pledged to hinder the forwarding of troops, and only to do so when compelled by the Federal Government. A draft is the only way that the latter can compel the service of the citizens, and then look out for trouble, for we have our plans all arranged under such circumstances.

November 6, 1862.—General McClellan removed from command. Bad, very bad for us.

November 8, 1862.—The Government seems resolved to revenge their losses at the elections, by retaliating on all pro-slavery officers in the army. Several have been removed from their positions, and more than one has been ordered before a Court Martial. Our power to prevent this is worse than weak—we are, in fact, powerless now.

November 16, 1862.—So Lincoln has turned religious as well as an autocrat. The army are to go to prayer at his command. He assumes to be at the head of the Church as well as the Divided States. Well! We shall see how it will work.

November 18, 1862.—Have just received news from Richmond that President Davis intends to practice retaliation. He has proclaimed that if General McNiell is not given up, he will hang ten prisoners. That is the only way now. What does he intend to do with Butler?

[As this proclamation of Jefferson Davis was dated in Richmond on November 17, this shows clearly that Surratt must have had a much more open communication with the Rebel Government than could be obtained by even the officers of the U. S. Army.

The remainder of the entries for this month are merely records of the movements of the army towards Fredericksburg, and personal remarks on the prospects of a battle. He also alludes to the hopes the people of the South had in the effect that will be created by the operations of the Confederate cruiser " 290 " or Alabama. The dates under which all the various entries are made would show that he must have had secret information of these facts, as they were unknown at the time to the general public.—EDITOR.]

December 15, 1862.—The invincible Army of the Potomac has been beaten again. Once more our schemes are working well. It was not accident that caused a certain order to go astray, and the result has justified the means. Brother —— did well in that affair.

I wonder how the merchants of New York like the Alabama now? Perhaps a few repetitions of such doings as have just been reported will cool their enthusiasm for carrying on the war. The California steamer was a good prize.

The people look gloomy over the affair at Fredericksburg. They will look worse before the year is out. The South has been apprised of all the intended movements of this present campaign season, and if they are not all defeated it is because the Confederate army has not the necessary strength. Grant's proposed movement will fail without doubt. Our Order can and will defeat that before a week is over. Rosencrans' movement will not succeed either.

[As this entry was apparently made several days before the reverses took place, it is plainly shown that even the supposed secrets of the army were known to its enemies long before they were developed, and all movements were thus promptly met and checked. The surrender of Holly Spring took place on December 19, and the repulse at Haines Bluff on December 27. The disastrous battle of Murfreesboro took place on December 29, 30, 31; whereas this entry is all under the date of December 15. How did he gain his information? This is one of the most important questions to have decided—EDITOR.]

December 16, 1862.—Congress is having somewhat of a hard time of it, or rather, the Government party find that much dissatisfaction exists throughout the North as to their conduct. I wonder whether the American autocrat really intends to proclaim the slaves free on New Year's day. If so, the war will be carried on in a very blood-thirsty manner. The South will not submit to any such measures; and, as that course would ruin the planters, there is very little doubt but that a fearful and bloody retaliation will fall on the heads of those who attempt to carry it out. Booth told me to-day that, should such a measure be proclaimed, the life of him who proposed it would be in great danger. But latterly that man has become very vapory, and often repeats his Shakspearian quotation about " the Ephesian dome," &c. Still it is not the first time he has proposed to me to remove the despot by some violent means. But how?

[It will be seen that the foul deed of assassination had long been contemplated, and that, up to this time, the keeper of this Diary had looked upon it as a visionary idea; but that the poison had been instilled, and was now beginning to have effect, is very evident. Still there is no proof to be gathered from this record that, up to this time, Surratt had really resolved upon anything so desperate as a cold-blooded murder; although his constant acquaintance with Booth, his love of money, and his greed for notoriety might have engendered thoughts in his brain which, during calmer moments, he would not only have discarded but utterly repudiated. That aught like true patriotism for the South existed within his breast is really to be doubted—his predominating passion, as expressed in his diary, being money—EDITOR.]

December 18, 1862.—I start for Richmond to-morrow.

[There are no more entries in the Diary under the year 1862, which doubtless shows that he must have been away from home during that interval.—EDITOR.]

January 1, 1863.—The decree has been issued; the freedom of the slaves proclaimed. Abraham Lincoln! thy days are numbered!

CHAPTER X.

AFTER THE RESOLVE.

January 13, 1863.—Have had some conversation with Booth on the subject that so much interests us. He is crazy on that idea, and will make some rash attempt that will ruin all, unless he be diverted from his purpose. I do not like his fanatical fondness for that woman. She is leading him to his ruin, either one way or the other.

By the way I have made the acquaintance of as pretty a piece of muslin as can be found. I reckon she has taken a fancy to me, and if that fellow St. M——will only keep out of the way, there will be but little doubt of success. But I will not be such a fool as Booth. She shall never know my secrets. Good or bad, the best *confidante* is one's own breast.

January 14, 1863.—Saw Booth again to-day. He is wild on this new idea of his; and appears determined to venture something, no matter at what risk, in order to secure fame. They say he is a descendant of the famous Jacobin, John Wilkes; and, if so there will be but little doubt that he will be courageous enough to carry out the most impossible scheme. I do not believe he cares for either god or devil when bent upon a certain idea: if there is a mere shadow of success in the future he will pursue it, even to his own destruction. Impulsive in all things, he lets his feelings, not his reason, guide his actions; and, oftimes, by this very impulse, not only endangers himself, but the welfare of his best friend or relative. He cares little for money—it is all fame with him. Fame? Bah! What is it worth? Give me the gold. A man with plenty of gold can buy fame; without it, he may strive and struggle, and will die unknown, no matter what his talent may be. What is fame worth?

If living, perhaps it may gain a few dollars; if dead, nothing,—for he will soon be forgotten in this changeable world. Booth's famous quotation shows his mind:

"The daring youth who fired the Ephesian doom
Outshines in fame the pious fool who raised it." *

He says these lines are Shakspeare's; but I do not find them in any of the editions in the libraries. I do not know what possessed me to look for the quotation; but Booth has repeated it so often, that I could not resist the desire to search it out. I wonder whence Booth really got the lines. But it is of no value to me to know; it will bring no money to my purse. I have spoken to Booth, at times, about the necessity of getting plenty of money for doing such dangerous work.

"' 'Tis trash,'" said he, contemptuously, "'something, nothing.' Who would barter fame for money? Not I! Give me a fame that exists when money has perished."

He may think himself right; but give me money. With it, distance is nothing—it can be overcome; justice's eyes, said to be bandaged, can be completely blinded; and the most difficult scheme can be carried out. Money is all potent; it is everything! Let me but have money, and I will defy the law and even the world's opinion. I have no fear of the law if I have but money. The most upright Judge can be bought, for "every man has his price;" and if I have but money, the officers of the law might be within a yard of my place of concealment, and yet I should never be found. The world's opinion is always guided by the

---

* These lines are ascribed by many to Shakspeare; but, as is written in the Diary, they are not to be found in any of the orginal editions of that author's work. It is more than likely that they are an interpolation of the noted Colley Cibber, who arranged several plays for the stage.—EDITOR.

length of a man's purse, and the solidity of its contents. If a man be poor, he is at once criminal, no matter how innocent he may be; if rich, he may be as guilty as Satan, his well lined coffers will alter the "opinion" of his character. Such is the world! The contractor who robs the Government, and murders the poor soldier by means of polluted stores, is a gentleman—because he has made money. The honest man, steadily pursuing his onward course in search of fame, is guilty of anything of which his detractors my accuse him. Why? He has no money!

But, pshaw! I am turning moralist. As that is the case, it is time I ceased writing in my diary.

January 15, 1863.—Met to-day, in Washington, one of my old College mates, L. I. W——. I wonder whether he is to be trusted; if he is, perhaps, sometime or the other, he may be useful. He once seemed to be in favor of the Southern cause, and I believe still is. What times we used to have at College together. But, then, it is not wise to trust too many with our secret. Booth makes too many friends, and that is his weakness. We shall certainly want assistance; but it must be from those of whom there can be no doubt. In gaining such friends, as W——, and in their securing their co-operation, it will be far better that they know nothing of what is really intended. I have heard it said, that an innocent boy can pass a counterfeit bill better than those who have been engaged in the making of them. Therefore, I believe it the best to keep all those, who are not to take an active part in the affair, in perfect ignorance of the object intended. Perhaps it will be well to tell Booth of this idea; for in this way such persons as W—— may be induced to do more, and perhaps with greater success, than if they were made fully acquainted with all our secrets.

I wish Mother would move into Washington. We could there operate better. My constant going in and out of the city may excite suspicion some day. Besides they are getting cautious, and the sentinels question a little too closely after dark.

It is true, that I am pretty well known; but if we resided there, my moving about would not be considered so strange, and I could learn more. Perhaps, a little persuasion might induce her to adopt this course.

[It seems, by the foregoing, that Surratt was in the habit of writing his thoughts as they occurred, for many of his entries are more like reflections than a mere record of events. As he doubtless often wrote essays at College, that exercise gave him this habit, which in this case makes his diary far more valuable to the general reader.—EDITOR.]

January 16, 1863.—Spoke to mother to-day on the subject. She seems willing. Talks about opening a boarding-house. Says that she will have no Yankees to live with her. Seems to have some new idea in her mind, but will not tell what it is. Talks a great deal about the success of the Southern cause. Perhaps, she is planning something since she saw Mrs. S——from Richmond. It has been arranged that I shall carry dispatches between that city and Canada. Well! If it pay me, perhaps I might do worse. They must have some means of communication; and, as the coasts are blockaded, and the Yankee army keeps almost every known road closed up, it will require some one who knows the unfrequented paths to do the work. Mrs. S——says they are beginning to refuse passes by way of Fortress Monroe; and, since M. W. was removed from the War Department, it is difficult to get any to go back through the lines. If I undertake the work—and none I know of can do it better—the Confederate authorities must pay well for my services. Since the Abolition Proclamation, I find it more difficult than ever to persuade people against the Federal Government; although we have so worked upon their minds that is not so easy for them now to get volunteers as formerly, even at a high price as a bounty.

There is a great talk about a draft. Let Abraham I. only try it, and then we shall be able to do something again. While troops are gained without force, the people do not seem to care; but if they only attempt to make any of them go against their will, then will be the time to raise up the masses against the Government. The plans are all arranged.

[The date of this entry is in January, and is interesting when compared with subsequent events.—EDITOR.]

January 20, 1863.—Lincoln seems determined to carry out his Abolition policy. What was considered a crime in John Brown, and for which the old fanatic was hung with the calm approval of the North, is now being esteemed a rare virtue—why? Because he only attempted to free a few niggers, and Lincoln is making a wholesale job of the matter. Strange that vice should become a virtue, because more are engaged in it. But to kill a single man, makes the doer of it a murderer; to kill thousands, a hero. But such it is, and ever will be.

Our order is getting less powerful throughout the North. Perhaps this arises from the number that have gone South to join the Confederate service; and perhaps it is caused by the recent exposures which have made some afraid. The northern spies have done us a great deal of mischief; but yet we are not quite broken up. There is yet work for the daring to perform.

[For the next few months the entries are of a trifling character as connected with the operations of the winter; and it would almost appear as if he had not been engaged in anything that was considered worth recording. Occasionally there is a break between the dates, and an interval of several days in the record, as if the writer was absent during the time ; but the diary gives no clue as to his movements or operations. The proper authorities may perhaps be enabled to find out those facts at the right time.—EDITOR.

CHAPTER XI.

THE RIOT IN NEW YORK,

June 6, 1863.—After a great deal of trouble, we have contrived to excite a feeling among the Northern editors about the despotic rule over the Press. At first they refused to take any notice of the suggestions ; but the remarks, that were made at the time of the visit, have not been idly spoken. They are ripening now into good fruit, and there is to be a meeting of the Press to see what can be done. ——of the New York——says that if some united course can be agreed upon, the Government will have to yield.

June 9, 1863.—The meeting has been held in New York. Could not learn what they have resolved to do. Latterly our friends have had to be very cautious, otherwise they would lose their situations in the various affices. Our cypher dispatches are all stopped in the telegraph offices, no matter how skillfully written. The mails are not secure, and even private messengers are closely watched by the Government spies. But for——in the New York office, one of my despatches to ——would have been seized, and then what a discovery would have been made, since they have found out the key. It is my firm opinion that one of our party has turned traitor ; if so, and he should be found out, his life would not be worth much. Fortunately, only the tried and faithful know the plans now on foot, and no papers have passed likely to lead to a discovery of the facts.

June 10, 1863.———from Fortress Monroe has been here to-day, and held a consultation with——of New York. The latter takes on papers to that city to certain parties there. As both move with a semi-official character, no one would suspect them of being bearers of despatches from Richmond. Even the Government detectives are at fault this time.

[Here another interval in the dates takes place, but is explained by the next entry.—EDITOR.]

June 23, 1863.—How excited they are in Richmond now. I saw B——there, and he says that the movements now taking place will secure a victory without chance of failure, if those in the North will only do their duty. He little knows how our movements are trammelled, since the spy system was instituted.

June 24, 1863.—Received a message to-day from Richmond. Must go to Baltimore to see Booth, and then off to New York. There is work before us now.

[Another interval in the record here takes place.—EDITOR.]

July 3, 1863.—Had arranged everything in a manner that could not fail, as the militia had been sent away; but Mrs.——told me that——said the Government had been warned, and were prepared. The advance on Gettysburg would have made the opportunity a splendid one. Mrs.——told me plainly that I was suspected and watched; if so, it will be dangerous to go on again at present to New York, as the police are on the look-out for every person that is in any way doubted. How it is that she has escaped so long I cannot make out; but she lives in a very secluded place, and the family of an army officer occupies part of the house. None but those acquainted with her would suppose so quiet and secluded a person could be engaged in any scheme against the Government. She will be a valuable agent by-and-by, as indeed she now is in minor matters.

July 4, 1863.—Great rejoicing about the victory. Perhaps they may have cause for sorrow yet. If Vicksburg is lost, the South will, never will be able to rally against such disasters.

July 7, 1863.—Vicksburg *is* lost, and many in whom we have had faith for co-operation have become faint-hearted. If all else fail; then the South must be avenged.

July 8, 1863.—There is to be a draft in New York, and the people are greatly opposed to it. Mrs.——sent a messenger to me to ask if the former plan should be carried out if an opportunity served, and to telegraph, as she had agents waiting.

No time to visit Richmond, and after consultation with Booth and——answered in the affirmative, but re-commended the greatest caution.

July 9, 1863.—Visited Baltimore to-day and sent on fifty men to New York. Had great difficulty to get them out of the city in consequence of the martial law. All suspected persons were refused passes, there-fore our best men will be absent. By taking different tickets, some for Boston, Philadelphia, Trenton, New York, New Haven and other places, they were all en-abled to leave the city without suspicion. Provided them with the means to purchase other tickets at the places where they stop. The first draft takes place on Saturday, so they will have plenty of time; and when they get to New York, they are to scatter themselves among the poorer classes throughout the city. The militia are still absent chasing up Lee. They will never catch him. He will be in Virginia again before two days are over.

July 11, 1863.—Draft commenced to-day in New York. The men have all arrived. Mrs.——tele-graphed that "they have got work." All right. There is no chance for similar operations here. Have

tried Philadelphia and Chicago ; but both will fail unless New York succeeds. Arrangements have been
made in those places, and they have only to get the signal from New York to begin work in earnest.

July 12, 1863.—Mr.——of the Washington *Chronicle*
says there is a great feeling in New York in opposition
to the draft. All appears to work well.

July 13, 1863.—The work has commenced in earnest.
The city of New York is in a state of riot. All the
wires have been cut, and news has to be brought some
miles to be sent on here. Philadelphia is disturbed,
but the authorities have had time enough to get ready
before anything effectual could be accomplished. Have
not heard from Chicago.

July 14, 1863.—Could get nothing decisive from
New York about today's proceedings. The New York
papers are full of yesterday's affair. From the contra-
dictory reports therein it would seem as if the authorities were paralyzed ; if so, all will work well.

July 15, 1863.—Bad management. Where could——
have been. He was to have taken the lead in the affair
at New York. As it is, there has been no organization in the matter, and the best laid plan has failed.
The Government have ordered on a number of Regu-
lars to New York, and the militia are also returning.
In Chicago the whole thing failed, and in Philadelphia
it was no better. Trusting to others, and this is the
result. But my part has been well attended to, and
therefore no blame can rest on me. This failure may
ruin all.

[From this entry onward there seems, for a time, to
have been no regular record kept, as if he had given up
all idea of carrying on a diary. Even his heretofore careful notes of army operations were neglected ; perhaps,
disheartened at the constant reverses of the South, he
had resolved to keep no account of them. His former
entries of army movements spoke very sparingly of reverses, and brilliantly of successes of the Confeder-

ates ; but after this date, the movements generally mentioned are those of Mosby, Morgan and other guerrillas. He praises the skill of Morgan in crossing the Ohio river; but condemns him for allowing his forces to be captured. He also blames Toombs for betraying the poor condition of the Confederate Treasury. Under date of Nov. 28, 1863, he records the escape of Morgan from the Ohio Penitentiary, but makes no further remarks. In fact the diary for about twelve months is both dull and uninteresting to any one but himself.—EDITOR.]

CHAPTER XII.

PLOTS AND PLOTTERS, ETC.

July 4, 1864.—The North—The cruel, blood-thirsty North—will find that in spite of all its boasts and glorifyings, the South is not yet dead. Lincoln may advance his Hessian troops on every side ; but still he will find a determined foe. It may take strongholds and capture cities ; but that does not end the war. While there is a man in the South, that man will fight. They will not conquer the South, much as they may rejoice to-day. We have yet a hope that the Democratic party of the North will do us justice, and, in the coming election, show Abraham Lincoln that his usurpation and despotism is displeasing to the people. The gallant men in the Shenandoah Valley are already advancing, and once more will occupy the soil on the north of the Potomac. Already is Mosby across, and he will not return without inflicting some injury on the Yankees. Let him but advance on Washington, he will find true friends to welcome him here.

[From this date he regularly records the movements of the Confederate forces, the defeat of Wallace at the Monocacy, the plundering operations of Mosby's band, the capture of Winchester by Ewell, and other affairs which are now matters of military history. He regrets, on one occasion, that the military rule in Washington had prevented him from giving some information— what he does not state—to certain parties in New York, by which means he had hoped to have given aid to those who were then threatening the capital. He glories over the capture of General Franklin, but blames the raiders for letting him escape after having so valuable a prize in their hands. He speaks in glowing terms of the schemes that were being put into practice by a Dr. B., asserting that they would create more destruction among the Union troops than the bullets of the Confederates. As nothing further is said about the doctor, it can only be surmised that he refers to the dastardly yellow-fever plot that created such destruction in Newbern, and was to have spread also throughout Washington. He praises the gallantry of the raiders, and also records in glowing terms their escape, and subsequent operations in the Shenandoah Valley; but when he hears of Farragut's success at Mobile, although not then confirmed, and records the appointment of General Sheridan to the command of "the valley," together with the arrival of fresh troops, he does so in language that indicates a disheartened feeling, and looks upon the latter as "worse than a failure." This brings the diary down to August 7, 1861.—EDITOR.]

August 8, 1864.—Have heard from City Point. Tom, who enlisted in the —— regiment, writes that he will do some good work to-morrow. Says it may cost him his life; but hopes to "send Grant and his staff to h—." That would be a victory indeed.

August 9, 1864.—No news from Tom to-day.

August 10, 1864.—Tom succeeded in blowing up the

boat yesterday; but perished himself in the attempt.
Grant and the rest all escaped. It was a bold attempt; but the fuse was too short, and the explosion
premature. All our best schemes fail lately. It looks
like a fatality. Hope the Canada movement will do
better.

August 12, 1864.—Failed again. The movement
from Canada has not been well carried out. Surely
that could have been successful. Everything goes
wrong now.

[The entries under dates between August 13 and
August 23, are merely records of current events, and
a statement that he had visited Richmond; but
no remark is made as to the object of that visit. The
next important record is the following: EDITOR.]

August 29, 1864.—McClellan and Pendleton are
nominated. Should they be elected, it would be
worth a dozen victories, and would repay for the loss
of Vicksburg and Chattanooga. And if McClellan
fails to aid the South, he can easily be put out of the
way to make room for Pendleton. Now is the time for
the order to work and secure their election.

August 30, 1864.—Received a dispatch to-day from
Canada. Should have started but was warned to be
cautious. Shall leave to-morrow.

[Here one of those breaks that we have before
noticed takes place in the Diary, and is explained by
subsequent entries.—EDITOR.]

September 6, 1864.—Have learned something this
trip at any rate; and, if only successful, we will bring
the war home to the hearths of the Northerners, and
cause them to feel a little of what the South has suf-
fered. The cities of Boston, Philadelphia and New
York are to be burned; a raid is to be made from
Canada upon the shipping of the lakes, and a force of
men are to rush across the border and attack the
frontier towns. The prisoners at Johnson's Island are
also to be released, and join in the affair. The princi-

pal parties who are to engage in this work are now in Canada, and I have seen the leaders. The whole of this grand scheme is to be carried out on the same day, if possible, so as to create an universal panic, and to make the people call on the Government for peace. There has been other projects spoken of, but the Confederate Government has not yet agreed to them, being willing to abide by the result of this project first. Mrs. —— and her sister are to take an active part in the firing of New York; and, when I told her of it, she seemed almost mad with joy. She asserted that if it were possible she would like to make New York, like Grant has declared the Shenandoah Valley shall be, if the war continues, "a desert waste." How she curses Grant and Seward, and is not very choice in her remarks about Sheridan. Well! Perhaps she has had cause.

September 7, 1864.—So the news has reached Washington that Morgan has been killed and his band routed. If the Canadian scheme is successful, that death, with the many others of good Southern men, will be fully avenged.

Sheridan is moving again, and this time he carries a torch as well as a sword. Let them burn away; the South will meet fire with fire.

September 8, 1864.—No news yet of the proposed scheme. It cannot have failed. What can cause the delay?

September 12, 1864.—Have been on to New York. Have learned that they have received instructions to to await more direct orders from Canada, before commencing the work. The movement on the lakes is to be tried first. It would have been better to have carried it out all at one time; but it is feared that they have not sufficient force to engage in all the enterprises. Have received despatches to that effect for Richmond.—

[Here another interval takes place in the dates;

indicating plainly an absence from his home.—EDITOR.]

September 20, 1864.—So Beall has carried out a part of his programme; but the principal movement at Sandusky failed from some cause. Surely there has been no treachery. Beall has, however, done well, and the movement has created a diversion. If the prisoners at Johnson's Island had only been released, we might have had a good fighting force at full liberty on the Northern frontier. Something must have gone wrong in the matter.

Should the elections fail us, we shall have to resort to some more efficient method to get rid of Lincoln.

Sheridan has completely beaten our forces in the Valley, and is marching onward in triumph. The left of the Confederate army is ruined.

[The record is now again for a time without interest, except as a journal of current events, and Surratt seems to have been merely an idle spectator. Occasional breaks in the Diary indicate absence from home; but nothing is written to say how he had been engaged.—EDITOR.]

CHAPTER XIII.

RAIDS, AND OTHER PLOTS RECORDED.

November 3, 1864.—The prospects each day grow worse and worse with regard to securing the election. Lincoln has resolved to be again elected, and is sending home the troops to vote for him. If a man can get a thirty days' furlough for merely recording his vote for "Uncle Abe," as they call him, of course they will take the leave of absence so as to be able to see their friends.　The feelings of the people are changing with the victories, and our chances have been lost.

November 5, 1864.—New York seemed almost certain for us, and we counted on her; but a change in the programme of Lincoln may lose us that city, as there is some military movement going on that neither Booth nor I can readily make out.　W——, who is living with us, says, he can gain nothing direct on the subject, although in one of the Departments.

It was intended to have given the so-called American Metropolis a warming on election night; but I am afraid the plan will be frustrated.　However, the order is to come from Canada, not from me.

November 6, 1864.—Butler has been ordered to New York City.　What for?　Is our plan known?　It would be useless to attempt anything while he is there.　"Watch and wait" must be our motto for the present.

November 7, 1864.—Prospects worse than ever.　The only hope the South ever had of late will certainly now fail her.　The Knights are powerless either to aid or lead.

November 8, 1864.—The election returns are in, at least enough to decide that McClellan is defeated.　To save the South, Lincoln must be removed before the 4th of March.　He shall *never* again be inaugurated. Booth wants his life, but I shall oppose anything like murder.　It would serve our turn quite as well to capture the despot, and keep him for a while in Libby Prison.　I reckon the South would then gain the day.

November 9, 1864.—It is nearly time we heard from Panama.　If those engaged in the work can only succeed in securing one of the Pacific steamers, she can be armed and operate in fine style in those waters. This movement, with our schemes from Canada, &c., will paralyze the North for a time; during which period Congress may be made to pass a law in our favor.　Co-operation is everything.

November 10, 1864.—The armies are going into Winter quarters; the dreaded Butler has left New York, and now is our time to begin. I must leave for Canada to-morrow for instructions.

[Here succeeds a break in the record of dates.—EDITOR.]

November 23, 1864.—Have seen T——and McD—— in Canada. The work is to commence at once. S—— says I am to remain at Washington and operate thence, if an opportunity can be found. I would have liked to have been engaged in the New York work; but it is thought in Canada that I should do better here.

I wish W——would not be so inquisitive. He somewhat cripples my movements. But he is very useful in getting those despatches, and I put him off, when he inquires about how I get my money, by telling him that I am mixed up with certain cotton speculations.

November 23, 1864.—Am getting anxious lest our scheme should fail. What an illumination to greet *our* last victory. And the North will have to pay for the bonfire.

November 25, 1864.—A telegram just received from Mrs.——that " Rob. and his men have work, which is expected to pay well." Good! Then this night will tell the tale.

Nearly midnight and no news. New York ought to be brilliantly lit up before this. What is Mrs.—— about? Why has not Rob. telegraphed.

November 26, 1864.—Failed again. Every one of them failed. A scheme so well planned, so finely located, and so skillfully divided among just enough to keep the whole thing secret, and yet to have failed. We must have had traitors among us. So good a thing could not have miscarried, but by design.

The Border operations may succeed better; and if Charley only burns up Butler in the Greyhound that will be a good revenge.

Every failure which may attend our operations now, will add all the more to the final day of reckoning, when the Western wood-chopper will have to pay up for all the short comings.

[Another break in the diary.—EDITOR.]

December 10, 1864.—The Richmond authorities are far from pleased at the course things have taken, and threaten to stop the supplies unless something more definite is carried out. Have despatches ready for Canada.

It is painful to see the desolation of Virginia. War is indeed cruel. But the South will hold out while there is a man left. The North by superior strength may subdue for the time; but they will never conquer the descendants of the Cavaliers.

Butler escaped. "The devil always looks after his own."

Mother and Booth are getting very intimate, and she appears to be engaged in something that is not yet clear to my mind. She had better keep out of any of his wild schemes; they are barely practical, and he who undertakes them must perish.

[The record breaks here again.—EDITOR.]

December 16, 1864.—There is much excitement in Canada about the St. Alban's affair. The daring fellows had been arrested; but by some local flaw they were discharged. The Canadian Government have ordered their re-arrest; but have allowed them all the time necessary to make their escape before doing so. It will be difficult for them to get such evidence as will cause a conviction before a law court. Besides, the money they secured will pay for good legal assistance in the matter, and there are plenty of lawyers in the Province whose influence would be enough to override, before a jury, any testimony the Yankees might bring. General Dix may issue orders; the Canadian Government may "arrest the raiders," and all show of law may be carried out; but not one of the brave

fellows who entered St. Alban's, will ever be con
victed.

December 20, 1864.—The Governor General o
Canada has just sent a dispatch that the officers of the
law have succeeded in securing one of the St. Alban'
raiders, as they are called. They will not dare to pun
ish him for any breach of neutrality. Besides, all thi
apparent activity on the part of the Government of the
British Provinces, is only show, to prevent any retalia
tion as set forth in General Dix's order.

[The records for the remainder of the year are un
important in connection with any movements of the
rebel party. The writer alludes to the operations o
the Canadian Parliament on the Neutrality question
and calls it a pretty attempt to cover up an actua
scheme to aid the Southern cause. " If," says he " the
South should really gain the day, the British wil
claim their do nothing acts as worth more than oper
assistance."—EDITOR.]

New Year's Day, 1865.—Another year begun, anc
still we struggle on with no hope beyond despair, anc
none to aid us. Why will not the proper authoritie:
agree to our plans. We must have money to carry
them out, and none can be got without the consent hac
and obtained from Richmond. Lincoln once in our
hands, and hurried off to Richmond ; then we coulc
dictate far better terms than any others could do.

January 10, 1865.—Visited Richmond again. Have
seen ————. Have proposed our plans, and received
a partial assent ; to be only carried out when all else
fail. Every effort to secure an honorable peace is to
be first tried. That course is of no use, in my opinion.
Old Blair has gone on to Richmond, and perhaps
something may arise from his visit. I believe President Davis would send Commissioners if Lincoln
would only meet them. If he does, and they fail to secure
the desired end, then our project is to be carried out.

January 15, 1865.—Booth and Mudd were with me

today at the " National." That fellow W—— was there. I would like to trust him, but dare not. We have planned out the roads to be taken, if we only succeed in capturing Lincoln. Booth is indignant at the imbecility of the Confederate Government. So far, I believe he is right, and agree with him that, if a blow is to be struck, it should be an effective one, and one that will make a lasting mark. Booth thinks we should do well to take Mother into our confidence, as I am so often away. I do not believe in women; but in this case, perhaps, it would be better. She could assist us greatly if she is mindful and willing. Must leave for Canada tonight; but I know nothing can or will be allowed to be done without the consent of the Confederate Government. The money-agent at Montreal is far too cautious to risk anything, unless there is a possibility of success, except on endorsement from the proper authorities as to the expenditure of the necessary funds.

January 25, 1865.—Have communicated the reply received at Richmond to the proper parties in Canada. They agree with us that such delays are bad, and that a good opportunity may be lost by such a waste of time. They have no faith in Peace Conferences; neither have I. Such attempts, if they fail, will only make the Yankees strike the blow the harder; for, it must be acknowledged, they have the power, and if the South can obtain no outside assistance, she must fall. The capture of Fort Fisher is the most serious injury the South has received during the whole war. They are now hemmed in by a wall of fire and steel. Blair has returned, and the Commissioners are to be met—at least that appears to be generally believed, as the old gentleman has gone on again to Richmond.

January 27, 1865.—Blair is back again. Now we shall soon see the end of all, or the beginning of worse. Lincoln had better be wise or he will have to pay the penalty.

January 30, 1865.—The Commissioners have arrived—so the telegraph operator tells me.

February 1, 1865.—Lincoln and Seward have both left to meet the Commissioners at Fortress Monroe.

CHAPTER XIV.

THE FIRST PLANS AND THEIR RESULT.

February 4, 1865—It is all over. Lincoln and Seward have returned, and there is no peace. The Governor-General of Canada has also signed the bill to prevent raids across the border. We are to perish, and none will help us! The cause is deserted by God and man. Every plan has failed. Now, perhaps, we may hope for the success of *our* movement, for it is only by that that the South can save herself.

February 6, 1865.—How disheartened the Southern papers read. " Sherman is riding rough-shod over the whole South, carrying destruction everywhere." This shall be terribly avenged by-and-by.

[The remainder of the entries during February are mere simple records of current events, with an occasional, but slight comment on them, but signifying at the same time that it "would all be right before the end" was over.—EDITOR.]

March 1, 1865.—The inauguration must take place. There are no means of reaching him before. The best laid scheme seems blocked on every side. But the opportunity will yet come. Well, better late than never.

March 2, 1865.—Have arranged all our plans, and secured the desired assistance. Booth is desperate; so are the others. They all seem ready to do anything to secure success. I don't think that young fellow Harold has much courage; but, then, he may be made of use by-and-by. The risk is great, but the reward greater. We have all we want for the work—everything except the opportunity.

March 3, 1865.—Too closely surrounded by his friends. No chance before the inauguration. The city is full, and all the office-seekers are buzzing around him like so many bees. Can't yet be done.

March 4, 1865.—The inauguration is over, and nothing done yet. My hopes and prospects rest solely on this attempt, and should it fail, I am ruined for ever.

March 5, 1865.—Lincoln attends a review on the 7th. We have it all arranged now, and nothing can fail. He goes out unattended, and we shall be enough—seven of us. The suddenness of the whole thing will prevent any attempt at rescue until it is too late. And once safely in Richmond, the independence of the South is certain, and my fortune made.

March 6, 1865.—All is prepared. Tomorrow afternoon!

March 7, 1865.—Ruined! my prospects blighted! The whole thing has failed! How was it that the route was changed? After having everything so finely planned.—I could blow out my brains.—Pshaw! what am I writing? That fellow, Louis, is always around when he is not wanted. I nearly betrayed everything this evening. But to think of so fine a plan going astray, and in such a manner. Could he have been warned? Oh, no! Our usual bad luck, that's all! Curse it! But for this mishap, the affair could not have failed; and by this time we should have been on the road to Richmond. We shall never again have such a chance.

[The foregoing three entries can perhaps be better explained from the following extract from the evidence of Louis I. Wiechman (the Louis, doubtless, alluded to above) given before the Military Commission during the trial of the Conspirators :—

During Payne's second visit to Mrs. Surratt's house, some time after the 4th of March, I retired from my office one day at half-past four o'clock; I went to my room, and ringing the bell for Dan, the negro servant, told him to bring me some water, and inquired at the same time where John had gone; he told me Massa John had left the front of the house, with six others, on horseback, about half-past two o'clock; on going down to dinner I found Mrs. Surratt in the passage; she was weeping bitterly, and I endeavored to console her; she said, "John is gone away: go down to dinner, and make the best of your dinner you can;" after dinner I went to my room, sat down, commenced reading, and about half-past six o'clock Surratt came in very much excited: in fact, rushed into the room; he had a revolver in his hand—one of Sharp's revolvers—a four-barrelled revolver; a small one, you could carry it in your vest pocket; he appeared to be very much excited; I said: "John, what is the matter, why are you so much excited?" he replied: "I will shoot any one that comes into this room; my prospect is gone, my hopes are blighted;" in about ten minutes afterwards the prisoner Payne came into the room; he was very much excited, and I noticed he had a pistol; about fifteen minutes afterwards Booth came into the room; and Booth was so excited that he walked around the room very frantically and did not notice me; he had a whip in his hand; I spoke to him, and recognizing me, he said; "I did not see you;" the three then went up stairs into the back room, in the third story, and must have remained there about thirty minutes, when they left the house together; on Surratt's returning home, I asked him where he had left his friend Payne; he said Payne had gone to Baltimore, and Booth he said had gone to New York; the negro boy afterwards told me that of the seven men who had gone out riding that afternoon, he said one was Massa John, and Booth, and Port Tobacco (Atzerodt), and that man who was stopping at the house, whom I recognized as Payne; though they were very much excited when they came into the room, they were very guarded indeed; Payne made no remark at all; those excited remarks made by Surratt were the only ones made; Surratt once made the remark to me that if he succeeded in his "cotton speculation," his country would lose him forever, and that his name would go down green to posterity.

The following is also an extract, taken from the evidence of John M. Lloyd, who kept the house formerly occupied by Surratt. The hiding place pointed out in the evidence is doubtless the one mentioned in the first part of the Diary, when he writes about concealing the papers where they could not be discovered :—

I reside at Mrs. Surratt's tavern, Surrattsville, about eleven miles from Washington; some five or six weeks before the assassination of the President, John H. Surratt, David E. Harold, and G. A. Atzerodt came to my house ; Atzerodt and Surratt drove up to my house in the morning first, and went towards Tee Bee, a post office about five miles below there ; they had not been gone more than half an hour when they returned with Harold ; John H. Surratt then called me into the front parlor, and on the sofa were two carbines, with ammunition, also a rope from sixteen to twenty feet in length, and a monkey wrench ; Surratt asked me to take care of these things, and to conceal the carbines ; I told him there was no place to conceal them ; he then took me into a room in the back part of the building and showed me where 1 could put them, underneath the joists of the second floor ; Mr. Surratt assisted me in carrying them up stairs, with the cartridge boxes ; I put them in there according to his direction ; Surratt said he just wanted these articles to stay for a few days, and he would call for them.

Taking these sworn statements in connection with the record in the Diary, it would appear that it had been the intention of Surratt and his companions to have captured the President and have taken him prisoner to Richmond, but that the whole thing failed by the driver of the President's carriage taking another road to the place where the review was to be held. The first project was evidently not assassination ; and that it only arose from the constant failures that a desperation ensued which ended in a cruel, cowardly murder.

For several days not a single entry appears in the Diary, the wretched man apparently not feeling any inclination to record the whole of the failure that he mentions in such a broken and excited manner. The interest, however, is not lost in the document even at the point where it is resumed.—EDITOR.]

CHAPTER XV.

THE ASSASSINATION.

March 17, 1865.—Goods news at last. Mrs. S.—— has arrived at our house from Richmond. She told Mother that she was the bearer of the most important dispatches from that city for the Confederate agents in Canada; that there was no time to be lost, and that, if the South ever hoped to succeed, it was in the belief that we would faithfully carry out the plans that she brought with her. We shall yet have some serious work to perform.

Saw Booth to-day, and introduced him to Mrs. S—. After a few minutes conversation with her, John came to me with his eyes dancing with unusual and almost unnatural brilliancy. What could he have learned from her?

March 18, 1865.—Booth called to-day and told me that he had gotten together in Washington all who were necessary for the purpose intended; that they could be ready at a minute's notice. He had a long conversation with Mother, at the end of which he said that "if anything was to be done, it should not be delayed, otherwise it would be too late." He declared his intention of going on to New York at once to perfect matters.

Mrs. S.——left for Canada to-day.

March 19, 1865.—Secured rooms for "Wood" at the "Herndon." That is as good a name as any other for him to go under here. W—— and I went together. It was a good idea that we had of saying the rooms were wanted for a sick man—his non-appearance at table will not therefore excite suspicion. If seen, he would not be thought very delicate in health.

Booth left to-day for New York. We agreed upon a first rate cypher to send by telegraph, so that we might know what each other was doing, without letting any one else into the secret. All seems likely to go on well.

March, 20, 1865.—Wood, the Doctor and Port Tobacco met me to-day at the place appointed. They are all ready to co-operate at the proper moment, so that the plan cannot fail time; and the very boldness of the movement will strike terror in those around, this and prevent any one from coming to the rescue. All goes well.

March 21, 1865.—No news yet received from Booth. I do not understand this. What can he be doing?

Wood was at our house to-day. We had a long chat up in my room over matters in prospect. He showed me the spurs, bowie-knives and revolvers that were to be used if required to carry out our affair. The weapons are all first class, and Wood seems just the right kind of fellow to use them to advantage. He is both powerful and desperate.

While we were engaged with our conversation, that fellow W——must poke in his nose. I felt like being uncivil to him; but thought it might excite suspicion. I am afraid he will yet suspect something; and then, by some blundering remark, upset the whole thing.

March 22, 1865.—Mrs. S.——is expected to return to-day from Canada. She wishes to go back to Richmond at once, and I am to drive her and Mother down to the Point to-morrow, so that she may meet Howell who is take to her across.

March 23, 1865.—Mrs. S.——has not yet arrived.

Received a dispatch to-day from Booth. How well the cypher works. Who could tell that so important a secret was concealed under the simple message. "Tell John to telegragh number and street at once." W.——wanted to know what particular number and street was meant. This made me angry at his continual questionings, and I said, hastily, "Don't be so damn'd inquisitive." This offended him and he left me without another word.

Replied to Booth's dispatch.

March 24, 1865.—Mrs. S.——returned to-day from Canada. She starts to-morning early, to meet Howell at the Point.

[Here one of those usual breaks takes place in the diary.—EDITOR.]

April 3, 1865.—Have had an exciting time for the past ten days. We started on the morning of the 25th of last month. I drove Mother and Mrs. S——to the Point, but could find no one waiting to meet her there. Could not then tell the reason; but have since learned that Howell was captured by one of the police boats on the 24th, while attempting to cross the Potomac. There was no option in the matter, therefore I had to go with Mrs. S.——on to Richmond. What a condition that city is in. Everything so high that rich men have become poor, and those not so well off are starving. Booth, President Davis and Secretary Benjamin declared that Richmond should never be evacuated. Have brought on dispatches for Canada.

News has reached here that Richmond has fallen. That must be one of Lincoln's lying dispatches. The Confederate Capital will not be surrendered.

While taking oysters with W——, have learned as definitely as could be possible that Richmond has really fallen. If that should be true, it will be dangerous to have these papers about, and therefore will take them with me to a place of safety in Canada.

April 5, 1865.—Called on Booth here in New York. Told him not to be too hasty in carrying out the plan upon which we had agreed. Shall leave this evening for Canada.

April 6, 1865—Arrived here in Montreal to-day: Called at once on the Confederate agent, and handed him the dispatches I had brought from Richmond. He examined them and said:

"This makes the thing all right."

He then talked with me about our proposed plan of carrying off the President, Secretary of State and other officials, and said that the Confederate authorities had consented to the movement. He added that he hoped we should make a sure thing of it. To-morrow I am to receive the necessary funds for the venture.

April 7, 1865—Called again to-day on the agent to get the money. He again conversed with me on the subject, listened to the plan we had proposed, and inquired as to the part I was to take in the matter. Gave him all the information advisable. Would have given him more, but that his Secretary seemed to be regarding me in a manner that I did not like. I am afraid too many know of this affair to warrant its success. Have not yet obtained the money.

April 8, 1865.—There seems to be no doubt now of the fall of Richmond; and it appears that Lincoln has been riding in triumph through the streets of the captured city. He may find such work dangerous. Glorying over the fallen braves! Cowardly triumph! He will yet pay dearly for that triumph! All is not yet lost while Lee's army remains in the field.

April 9, 1865.—Lee's forces are said to be in a very serious position, and cannot escape destruction if they continue to fight. But Lee is a wary general.

April 10, 1865.—Lincoln is again in Washington. Now is our time to act, and avenge the losses we have sustained on those who have caused them. Booth has written to me to say he has changed his mind, and wants my assistance in Washington.

It is rumored to-day that Lee has surrendered. That is impossible. The Yankees always set afloat these lying reports to operate on the Northern mind.

April 11, 1865.—Have received the necessary funds, and shall start tomorrow for Washington, to join Booth in his scheme.

The Yankee flag is to be raised over the battered walls of Fort Sumter on the anniversary of Anderson's surrender. If Lincoln should go down there, we shall miss our promised game. He must not be lost sight of.

[A break here takes place in the entries.—EDITOR.

April 15, 1865.—Lincoln is gone at last. Booth has carried out his oft-repeated threat, and has, so it is said, really taken the life of the tyrant. It seems too good to be true. But the "assassin"—Saviour—is being pursued. If he takes the road planned out, he will certainly escape. He has indeed gained an immortality of fame.

April 16, 1865.—My name is mentioned as connected with this affair. The States is no longer a safe place for me especially as Mother has been arrested.

[From this time forward the diary is very irregularly kept, at times full of records of events and passing thoughts, at others containing brief entries, with long intervals between them. Regrets and self praise, together with eulogies of the Confederates in Canada, &c., form the greater portion of the work, showing that, whenever distressed in mind or elevated in spirits, he generally relieved both, by writing in his Diary. Only those items that have been considered of general interest have been selected, in order to trace the career of the Conspirator, and to show the state of his mind from the time of the Assassination until the close of the Record. The rambling remarks and unimportant entries are therefore excluded.—EDITOR.]

CHAPTER XVI.

SURRATT IN CANADA LIVERPOOL AND EUROPE.

April 18, 1865.—Safe again on British soil, and under the protection of a neutral power. It will give them some trouble to find me here, and still more to take me; but to prevent accidental discovery I will disguise myself by dying my hair and staining my skin. I must remain here for a time, and when an opportunity offers sail for Europe.

April 19, 1865.—Montreal not safe ; left it, therefore, last evening. Detectives about everywhere. I shall not be looked for in this retired place.

I was foolish enough to make myself known to that stranger at St. Albans. Who knows but that he may have been one of the detectives ? In a case like this, caution is the best policy. I must be very careful.

What must be Mother's feelings at this time ? Herself in prison, and unaware of my safety. How did they discover her connection with the affair ? Some one must have betrayed her. Hope W—— has not been babbling.

Booth must have had some good reason for changing his plan, or he never would have done so. We had agreed on so good a scheme, that to change it seemed like tempting destiny.

April 28, 1865.—The Yankees are going to mock justice by pretending to try those whom they have captured. They cannot revenge themselves on Booth —he is out of their power. He died bravely, gun in hand, and without flinching. As for Harold, he was chicken-hearted, and deserves to be hung.

I wonder what is intended to be done with mother. Surely they will not hang a woman ! Should they do so, I will live only to bide my time.

May 11, 1865.—I find the Yankees are commencing what they call the trial with closed doors. Secret plottings to take the life of a few poor victims, and one a woman. The people and the press will cry such a thing down, or I am much mistaken.

I am safe here at any rate, under the protection of those professing my own religion. I have sought a sanctuary, and have found it. While here there is neither fear of betrayal, nor risk of discovery.

May 13, 1865.—News has just been brought to me that President Davis has been captured. If that be true, all our plans and dangerous risks have been in vain.

· *June* 1, 1865.—The trial drags on its weary way, and they are trying to take evidence condemning me as well as the rest—for I feel convinced they are all doomed.

June 30, 1865.—It is said the trial is over, and the evidence so strong that none will escape. What a narrow escape I have had. If taken in the States, my fate would have been settled long before this. What a fool W—— was to say anything about it. They could not have hurt him even if he had remained silent.

⊦ *July* 8, 1865.—They have hung my mother. Curse them! in every way curse them! She was no party to the mad freaks of Booth! She has been murdered by Johnson, but I will be even with them yet. After my sister pleading as she did for her mother's life, and yet they have hung her. Payne and Harold; well! they were in the plot; but then that cowardly fellow, Atzerodt, Johnson ought to have pardoned him, if even only because he was too cowardly to attempt to kill him. But they are all hung, and the rest have been sent to the Dry Tortugas. But, my mother! Curse them! curse them all!

[A very long interval takes place in the Diary, as if the writer was so much troubled by the reflections caused by the re-perusal of his last entry that he dare not record anything further of his own actions.— EDITOR.]

August 29, 1865.—All has been prepared for me to go to Europe, and I shall therefore bid a long farewell to that country for which I have risked so much—and in vain. I do not wish to die yet—I desire to live if only to make some parties suffer for having murdered my mother.

My disguise has so far been perfect, and even my best friends do not know me. It has been an easy thing, therefore, to elude the detectives sent to track me out, and I believe they have given up the search;

but still it will require some amount of both assurance and money to move about as safely among the Continental spies, if I am known there. Once ashore in France or Spain, and I shall fear nothing; until then, I feel as if in hourly peril. Perhaps I shall go to Rome—I shall be safer there than anywhere.

September 5, 1865.—Bade farewell to those kind friends who have so long given me a shelter. May their safety never be endangered, or their peace and happiness disturbed.

[The next entry appears to have been written on the steamer, bound for Europe, but has no date.—EDITOR.]

We had a fine voyage so far; but I cannot tell what distance has been traveled. Why do not these English vessels issue a bulletin, as on board those of the American service. It would be a great accommodation to know how we are getting along.

I wonder who the man is that sailed with me from Montreal to Quebec. He seems to have taken a great interest in my behalf, and when he learned that I was Surratt, the Confederate, who had been through so much, he seemed both surprised and pleased. I recollect he asked me several questions, among which was one inquiring whether or not I had been connected with the killing of Lincoln.

"Not exactly that," I replied, "but I have been concerned in a trick to carry him off. The plan was concocted by Booth and myself; but while I was in Canada, the main features were changed by Booth."

September 23, 1866.—Arrived at Londonderry, Ireland. Thought it necessary to go ashore in disguise, and, when in the city, found my precautions valuable, as a full description of my person had been sent to Europe in order to secure my arrest. Believed Londonderry safer than Liverpool for the first visit.

September 25, 1866.—Crossed over to-day to Liverpool. Found an asylum in the Oratory of the Church of the Holy Cross. My friends could not learn whether or not there had been any recent orders to secure my arrest, but still advised me to be cautious, at least for a short time, until I could get to the Continent.

[The movements of Surratt had, however, been closely watched up to this time, and official correspondence had passed between the various Consuls and the Secretary of State as to the advisability of arresting him; but after due consideration, and consultation with the Secretary of War and the Judge Advocate-General, it was, on October 13, 1865, decided "that no action should be taken in regard to the arrest of the supposed John H. Surratt at present." This doubtless explains how it was that John H. Surratt had been so long in Europe without being placed under some restraint.—EDITOR.]

October 1, 1865.—Arrived in London and presented my letters. All right.

October 3, 1865.—This England is a dull, heavy place. No amusement. I live, it is true, in a grand hotel; but it is not like an American hotel. There is no scarcity of money—it would not be wise for certain parties to let me run short. But this living in perpetual disguise is not very gratifying to my feelings. I do not like London, and will try the Continent

October 30, 1865.—V—— wishes me to go to Spain; but I preferred Paris, and therefore shall take my departure to-morrow. He will get the letters prepared by that time, and bring the funds.

October 31, 1865.—I start to-day; having received the proper letters of introduction to persons in Paris and seventy pounds in money. Now for a round of pleasure, if only to drown my senses, for the memory of my mother's death makes my life a misery. Were it not that I should put my own neck into a halter, I would send on to Washington the names of those who "aided and abetted" in the rebellion, and it will be found that they did not all belong to the Democratic party.

November 1, 1865.—Arrived in Paris. This is, indeed, a gay city. Hope the supply of funds will not run short.

November 2, 1865.—Conversed with Mr. A. to-day. He says Paris will ruin me, as I have already been recognized more than once. I think —— and the rest would like to get rid of me. They know that if I was out of the way, there would be none left to betray them. Although not the actual assassins, they had more to do with it than they would like known, especially ——, of New York. A—— wants me to go to Rome and join the Papal Zouaves. I could then be better protected, and money could reach me as well there as in Paris.

November 8, 1865.—My letters have gained me admission into the Zouaves. Surely I shall not be recognized here. In John Watson few would expect there existed the Confederate John H. Surratt.

[The subsequent entries are merely records of trivial events that occurred in the regiment to which he belonged, with occasionally a memorandum of money received from London, &c. While making an entry of a sum received from New York, he adds that " any refusal to keep up the supply will be attended by exposure, even if it may be necessary to go to New York for that purpose."—EDITOR.]

March 17, 1866.—How did that fellow St. M—— get into the Zouaves? He recognized me at once as the one who ran off with his girl. I shall have some work to keep his tongue quiet. He says that he did not care so much for the girl as to make it a point of a quarrel between us. I hope not. Still I would prefer not having been recognized.

[The next interesting entry bears the following date—the others being of a very trivial character:—EDITOR.]

April 15, 1866.—Have got into another mess with St. M——. It appears he was after some pretty Roman girl here, and my luck led me the same way. He tried his best, and I mine; but the result is he has come out a little the worse. I've got the girl, and he swears revenge. He can do nothing here against me; I am too well protected.

June 16, 1866—St. M——appears to be a better friend than before, and to have given up the idea of the girl; but yet, I am fully convinced he does not like being twice cheated thus by the same party. His whole talk is now about the late war and death of Lincoln. He seems anxious to know whether President Davis was connected with or not. That is a secret I will tell to no man, while I am safe myself; but if the Confederates desert me, then let them prepare for trouble.

[The entries next made, and for the next four months, refer principally to brief descriptions of the places where he was stationed, remarks on the girls, &c., &c. They are therefore omitted.—EDITOR.]

November 2, 1866—Have received warning of approaching danger. What can it be? Shall I fly? Where to? It may be fancy only, so I will stay and face it. I am too well protected to fear.

November 6, 1866.—Arrested! To be sent to the United States—what for?—the gallows? Perhaps too true! I am to die, but not unavenged. I leave these papers for my gallant companion, D——H——, with an earnest request that he will have them published in America. I will not be hanged—a better fate will be mine. I have often noticed the precipice. A leap down that will end my misery at once.

[Here the diary closes. Let the world judge between Surratt and his accomplices. The death of President Lincoln was certainly a cold-blooded assassination; but whether there were not others as guilty, in fact, if not in act, as those who have been stigmatized as the conspirators, is something that may be found out in the course of time. Should this be the case, it is to be hoped they may be justly punished—EDITOR.]

CHAPTER XVII.

SUBSEQUENT EVENTS—THE PERILOUS PLUNGE.

To complete the record, the editor has compiled the following facts, for which the writer of the Diary is not to be held responsible :—

Surratt was arrested on affidavit of a companion in arms given to Gen. King, the U. S. Minister at Rome, while he was serving in the Zouave regiment of the Pope ; and, on November 9, Cardinal Antonelli informed that official of the arrest and subsequent escape of the prisoner. The General at once notified Mr. Seward, adding that "As Veroli is close to the frontier, it is not at all unlikely that Surratt will make good his escape from his Zouave pursuers into the Italian Kingdom. I thought it well, therefore, to send a confidential person at once to Florence, to lay the whole case before the American Minister, and solicit his aid and that of the Italian government to the recapture ; for I did not feel at all sure that either a message by telegraph or a letter by mail, to Mr. Marsh, would, under the circumstances, escape the surveillance or possible interruption of the Papal authorities. I hope to have a report from my messenger within two or three days, and as Surratt was in his Zouave dress when he effected his escape, I think the chance a fair one that he will be retaken."

The following official despatch announced the escape :

" *To His Excellency the General, Minister of War, at Rome.*

" I received the following telegram from Captain Lambilly : At the moment of leaving prison, surrounded by six men as guards, Watson plunged in the Ravine (more than a hundred feet) which defends the prison. Fifty Zouaves are in pursuit. I will send your excellency the news which I shall receive by telegraph.

"The Lieutenant-Colonel ALLET."

The following official report gives the details of the
perilous plunge and escape :—

TO THE MINISTER OF WAR, ROME.

"FEROLI, 8th November.

"MY COLONEL : I regret to announce to you that notwithstanding
all my precautions, Jean Watson has succeeded in escaping. To
carry out the orders received, I had sent Sergeant Halyeril and six
men to Tresulti, where this Zouave was on detachment. They did not
find him there, for on that day Watson had asked leave to go to Feroli.
I charged the corporal of the third company, Vanderstracten, to take
him and turn him over to the post corporal Warren, to whom I had
already given all my instructions on the subject. All the measures ordered were carried out from point to point. Two sentinels, with
loaded arms, were placed, one at the very door of his prison, with orders to prevent any communication of the prisoner with anyone outside, and the other at the door of the barracks. The prison, and the
doors and windows, &c., had been inspected in the minutest details by
the locksmith of the common ; there was, therefore, nothing to fear in
that quarter. All passed off well until this morning at 4 o'clock.

"The prisoner was then awakened, and rose, put on his gaiters, and
took his coffee with a calmness and phlegm quite English. The gate
of the prison opened on a platform which overlooks the country. A
balustrade prevents promenaders from tumbling on the rocks situated
at least thirty-five feet below the windows of the prison. Beside the
gate of this prison are situated the privies of the barracks. Watson
asked permission to halt there. Corporal Warren, who had six men
with him as guards, allowed him to stop, very naturally, not thinking
he or the Zouaves present, that their prisoner was going to try to escape at a place which it seemed quite impossible to us to clear. This
perilous leap was, however, to be taken, and was crowned with success. In fact Watson, who seemed quiet, seized the balustrade, made
a leap and cast himself into the void, falling on the uneven rocks,
where he might have broken his bones a thousand times, and gained
the depths of the valley. Patrols were immediately organized, but in
vain. We saw a peasant who told us that he had seen an unarmed
Zouave who was going toward Caxa Mari, which is the way to Pied-
mont.   *   *   *   *   *   *

"Colonel of Detachments,

"DELAMBILLY.

"I have sent the description of this Zouave to the gendamerie."

As yet we have received no information of the ad-
ventures through which the rash conspirator must have
passed after recovering from the shock of his jump
over the precipice; but, doubtless, upon finding he had
escaped in so wonderful a manner, the love for life,
strong in every breast, induced him to make one more

attempt to elude the vengeance which was so surely pursuing him. He was traced from point to point through the Italian territory; but although the strictest search was made, he could not be found anywhere in that Country.

Intelligence having at last been received that a person answering the description given of Surratt had made his way to the City of Naples, General King at once placed the Consul on his guard, and the American fleet was called into service to prevent the escape of the accused man from any of the ports of the country. The warning was however given too late, and the fugitive was enabled to make good his escape, as will be seen by the following dispatch sent by the Consul at Naples to the one at Malta:—

"Surratt, one of the conspirators against Lincoln, left here last evening in the steamer Tripoli for Alexandria, under the name of Walters or Watson. He has on the uniform of a Zouave of the Papal States. The steamer stops at Malta to-morrow to coal. Have him arrested. If you do not receive this in ttme, telegraph to the Consul at Alexandria."

On December 2d Surratt was finally taken, and the following Cable despatch, announcing his arrest in Egypt, was received the same day by Mr. Seward:

" *To Seward, Washington :*
"Have arrested John Surratt, one of President Lincoln's assassins.
"No doubt of identity.   HALE,
                                                              " Alexandria."

The Admiral of the Mediteranean Squadron was then telegraphed to by Secretary Seward, and on December 17th, the " Swatara;" one of the U. S. Steamers, passed Malta on the way to Alexandria to bring the wretched man to Washington, for the purpose of taking his trial for complicity with those who caused the death of President Lincoln; and, on the 22d of the same month, the prisoner was placed on board the before-named steam corvette, in compliance with the orders received from the United States Government.

There has been much anxiety manifested by person
of different grades of society to mix up, with this sa
conspiracy, the name of Jefferson Davis. To those
as well as to others, the editor recommends a calm an
dispassionate perusal of the diary, with the hope tha
prejudice will be set aside for ever, and justice be don
to all parties.

The Editor in giving publicity to this document ha
had no intention of taking any particular side of th
question—either for the Government and against Sur
ratt, or for the accused againt his accusers. Those wh
desired the suppression of the diary doubtless had a
object in the matter, one that can better be explaine
by themselves than by the Editor of this volume.

The Diary is placed before the public in order t
show what the writer himself thought on the event
current of the late rebellion; and if it appears to con
demn him, or extenuate his conduct, every allowanc
must be made for the times in which it was written
and the exciting circumstances by which he was sur
rounded.

CPSIA information can be obtained at www.ICGtesting.com
Printed in the USA
BVOW09s2034120315

391515BV00006B/54/P